THE HORTICULTURAL CORRESPONDENCE COLLEGE

Little Notton Farmhouse
16 Notton, Lacock,
Chippenham,
Wiltshire SN15 2NF
Tel/Fax: **01249 730326**
Email: info@hccollege.co.uk
Website: **www.hccollege.co.uk**

PLANT PROPAGATION

Oliver Menhinick, Peter Brown & Andrea Callf

***Cyclamen coum* selections**
(1st summer after sowing)

'PLANT PROPAGATION'

© HORTICULTURAL CORRESPONDENCE COLLEGE
Little Notton Farmhouse,
16 Notton, Lacock,
CHIPPENHAM, Wiltshire
SN15 2NF
Tel / Fax: 01249 730326
Email: info@hccollege.co.uk
Website: www.hccollege.co.uk

Revised and Reprinted 2002.
Reprinted 2004.
This edition published by the Horticultural Correspondence College.
ISBN 0 9543550 0 8.
First published in 1994 by
Picton Publishing (CHIPPENHAM) Limited
ISBN 0 948251 74 3 under the title:
'Plant Propagation, Insight, Fundamentals and Techniques'.

Principal author and editor:
Oliver N. Menhinick, M.B.E., M.Hort.(RHS)., N.D.H.Hons. (RHS), M.Sc.(Bath)., B.A.Hons.(OU).,
F.I. Hort.

Designed and typeset by the Horticultural Correspondence College.
Printed and bound in the United Kingdom by:
Antony Rowe Ltd
Bumpers Farm Industrial Estate,
CHIPPENHAM
Wiltshire
SN14 6LH
Tel: 01249 659705

ABOUT THE HCC

The HCC offers its members the full tutorial care package that includes the marking of scripts and general care according to the details set out in the HCC's prospectus.

The HCC has as its "reason to be" a desire to be helpful. If the reader is not yet a member of the college and would like to join the roll of HCC members, then do please give the office a ring and ascertain what the current courses and fees are – or look at our website www.hccollege.co.uk. It is possible to purchase most courses at 50% off the rate but this is without the tutorial marking, and support package.

You can obtain a copy of our prospectus by ringing our Freephone number 0800 378918. For a more conversational approach, our office line is 01249 730326. This is also our fax number.

Acknowledgements to this 2nd edition.

To Peter Brown M.Hort of the University of Bath who made important contributions to the development of this edition to help the content meet the requirements of the RHS syllabus for their Advanced Certificate in Horticulture.

To Andrea Callf BSc.(Hons) who word processed the text, proof read and checked the HCC edition for use in our RHS Advanced Certificate series.

To Tricia Starling who prepared this text as it is in this edition, ready for issue as our 2002 annual prize book. [This tradition of prizes dates back to my first year in running the HCC. It marks the quality of the work submitted by the HCC student members].

Also to Deb Dixon for redrawing most of the illustrations.

Oliver Menhinick

CONTENTS

LIST OF ILLUSTRATIONS

Page

Figures:

Tables:

PLANT PROPAGATION - AN INTRODUCTION

Seeds represent a wonderful package – they contain life itself. They are relatively easy to store, to transport, to sow and to grow. Seeds are the result of sexual reproduction in flowering plants – sometimes involving flowers on separate plants of the same species. The great problem (if it is indeed a problem) is that the progeny may be variable. Seeds of wild species do come true, but even so in natural populations there is considerable variation – both in plant form and "productivity".

Over the millennia, civilisations have selected good forms of plants – so our carrots and onions are more productive – and ever since Napoleon's wife, the Empress Josephine, set about her rose garden at Malmaison rose breeders have endeavoured to raise even finer flowering bushes.

The great thing about vegetative plant propagation (as against raising plants from seed - seminal) is that the progeny come true to type – in colour, form and habit. Such progeny may also have a carry-over of pests and diseases.

There are five basic methods of plant propagation:

     (i)   by seed raising

     (ii)   by cuttings

     (iii)   by layering

     (iv)   by division

     (v)   by grafting

Each of these systems has their specialist methodology and it is rarely true to say that there is only one way to do something in plant propagation. However, this is not to say that it can be very useful indeed to stick to one reliable system.

In the present day we also have plant multiplication by tissue culture (micropropagation). This starts as a cutting in effect – a clean propagule grown in sterilised media under laboratory conditions.

Subsequent cultures of the tissue may be induced to produce further 'clean' cuttings and/or divisions when the plantlets have developed roots.

There is also gene modification. In some ways this represents what has been going on over the centuries - as in the production of a better carrot or rose – but what is new is the capacity to create plants with characters taken from plant families which are very different. There are risks associated with genetically modified (GM) crops, which are well flagged-up and publicised on TV, in the media and press.

However, we can probably agree that a woody strawberry bush - not unlike a potentilla (the same family) – would: save one's back when picking …also, maybe, keep the slugs off …and the chance of *Botrytis* be much reduced thanks to the better air circulation of the berries held aloft and away from the soil!

The "jury is still out" on GM crops, but it is so important one hopes that good scientific research is well to the fore of commercial exploitation, before the problematic implications, if any, are learned the hard way. (These problems might include aspects of our national health, plus the wild flowers and fauna that are our heritage.)

This lesson text will attempt to follow the pattern of the syllabus, using the following main headings:

1. Relevance of plant anatomy and physiology to propagation by seed.

2. Seed treatments.

3. Environmental factors affecting the germination of seeds.

4. Propagation by seed.

5. Relevance of plant anatomy and physiology to vegetative propagation.

6. Care of stock plants.

7. Use of propagation equipment.

8. Vegetative propagation.

9. Risk assessment.

[NB: The question of risk assessment is not one to be too easily dismissed because problems could occur. Some seeds are irritants, like *Capsicum* (peppers), and some plant tissue is poisonous, like *Oleander*. Some equipment is potentially dangerous, e.g. electrical services, so within the text we will also endeavour to identify safe health and working practices at all times.]

1. RELEVANCE OF PLANT ANATOMY AND PHYSIOLOGY TO PROPAGATION BY SEED

SEED STRUCTURE

Seeds of flower-bearing plants contain an embryo (from the fertilised ovum), a food store (cotyledons or endosperm) and a seed coat (plus, in many cases, a fruit wall). The embryo plant in the seed consists of a radicle, plumule, hypocotyl and cotyledons. A generalised seed structure, based on broad bean, is described below:

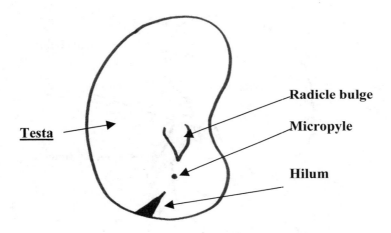

Figure 1: External structure of a Broad bean seed ** [see Note below]

The **testa** is the strong, outer protective coat of the seed; it may prevent water from entering the seed until germination occurs. Along the edge is the **hilum** – a scar that marks the region where the seed was originally attached to the fruit wall via a small stalk, the funicle, to the ovary wall. (Imagine a fresh pea pod, split open to reveal the peas inside attached to the edge of the pod by the funicle – see below.)

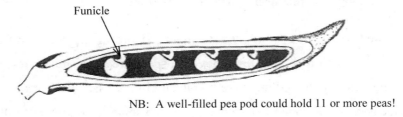

NB: A well-filled pea pod could hold 11 or more peas!

On the curved edge of the seed above the hilum is a bulge, which is the site of the radicle - the part of the embryo that develops into the first seedling root. The micropyle is a minute pore in the testa through which the pollen tube entered the ovule during fertilisation. It is at this point that water will enter the broad bean seed to commence the germination process. In many seeds the bulk of the water will enter via the testa, which may tend to behave like blotting paper.

Figure 2: Internal structure of bean seed
(the seed coat [testa] and one cotyledon   removed)

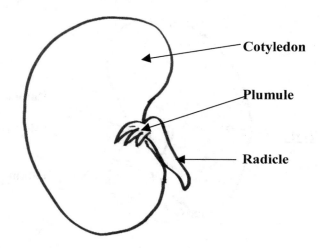

The **plumule** is the embryo shoot. Within the seed are two **cotyledons** (seed leaves) in dicotyledonous plants, but only one cotyledon in monocotyledons. The cotyledons may contain stored carbohydrates as in the broad bean, plus starch and proteins to support the seedling during germination and the early stages of growth. In some plants, for example maize, onion and ash, the cotyledons are very thin and small and food is stored in special endosperm tissue.

The stored foods, of course, also maintain the life of the seed until germination occurs. Although it is not all that obvious, seeds are alive and are respiring gently. This requires oxygen and there are two main bi-products - water vapour and carbon dioxide gas. Seeds do not live forever, although some seeds may last fully viable for many years.

Between the cotyledons and radicle is an area called the **hypocotyl**, the length of stem below the cotyledons.

[** NB: You are likely to come across similar drawings of broad bean elsewhere in our texts. Please do not be put off – have a go – identify for yourself the structure of seeds that you may have. Clearly, larger seeds are easier to see and draw so it may be that, initially at any rate, you look at: ash keys, sycamore seeds, lentil seeds, acorns, conkers, marrow or melon seeds, peas, almond, runner bean seeds; also orange and lemon pips (some of these are nuts and other fruits). It is sometimes jolly hard to work out the various bits – try a coconut! Nature in its variety is quite marvellous.

Sometimes more becomes obvious to the eye when the seeds are germinating. The old wet flannel system is very easy (see diagram below) and, while not wildly scientific, it can teach a great deal. In this case the objective is to watch the seeds swell as they absorb water. This may be followed by the emergence of the root and then the first stem or leaves.]

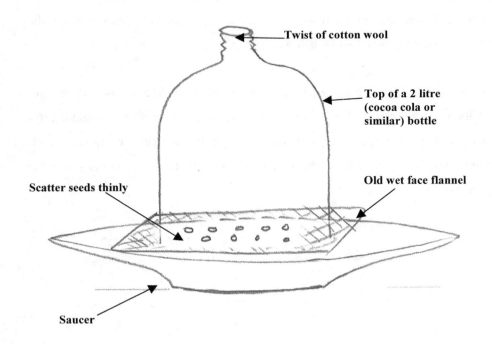

Twist of cotton wool

Top of a 2 litre (cocoa cola or similar) bottle

Old wet face flannel

Scatter seeds thinly

Saucer

THE GERMINATION OF SEEDS

At germination, the emergence of the radicle breaks a long period of inactivity and the embryo enters upon the most rigorous of physical and physiological changes that it will undergo throughout its entire life. The radicle grows into the soil, where it may absorb water and nutrients. It begins to develop side roots and the plumule pushes its way up through the soil and emerges into the air to become a green shoot bearing the first true plant leaves.

The structural changes which occur depend upon the nature of the germinating seed, whether there be one or two cotyledons and whether these come above ground during the process and whether the bulk of food is in the cotyledons or the endosperm.

The terms used to describe the mode of germination bear relation to the position of the cotyledons during the process. They may remain below ground or emerge above it. In the former case, germination is said to be **hypogeal** and occurs in broad bean, oak and grasses, for example. In the latter case, germination is **epigeal**, for example in ash, sunflower and onion. If the hypocotyl extends, the cotyledons emerge above the ground (see Figures 3 and 4 below).

It is to be noted that the emergence or otherwise of the cotyledons is often bound up with their special roles. They may, as in sycamore, proceed to assimilate carbon. Where endosperm is present, as in maize, the cotyledon may be much modified having a single role as a food absorber only and it remains below the ground (see Figure 5).

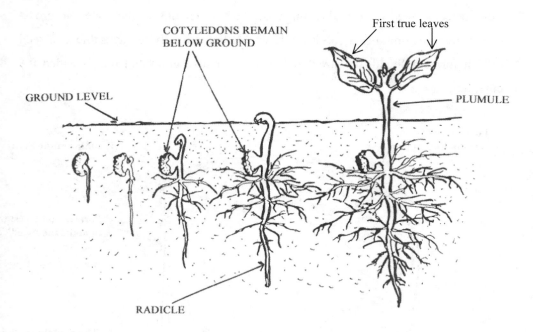

COTYLEDONS REMAIN
BELOW GROUND

First true leaves

GROUND LEVEL

PLUMULE

RADICLE

Figure 3: Hypogeal germination, as in Runner Bean

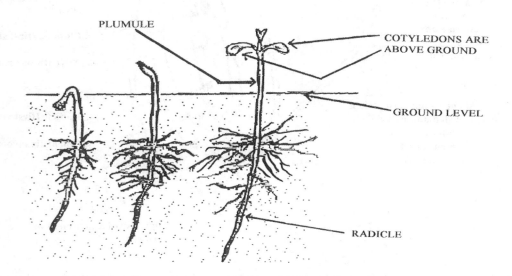

PLUMULE

COTYLEDONS ARE
ABOVE GROUND

GROUND LEVEL

RADICLE

Figure 4: Epigeal germination, as in Sunflower

Maize seeds - the grains - are really, botanically speaking, individual fruit because in addition to the seed there is the fruit coat and the remains of the style. In cross-section, the much-modified cotyledon is visible but is hardly recognisable as a seed leaf. It forms a shield-like structure inside the maize grain and this is called the scutellum.

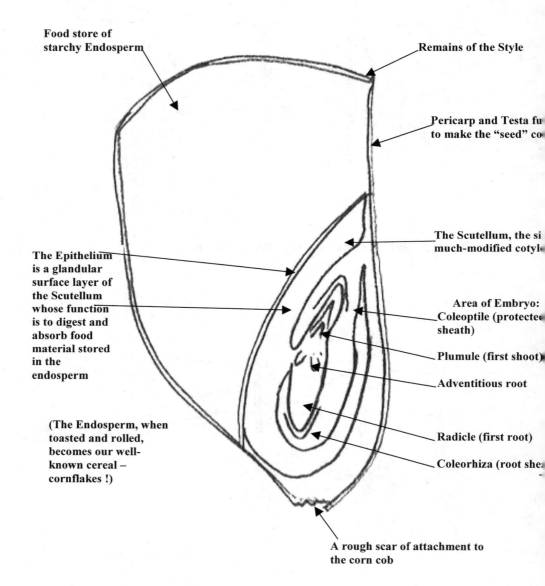

Food store of starchy Endosperm

Remains of the Style

Pericarp and Testa fu to make the "seed" co

The Scutellum, the si much-modified cotyl

The Epithelium is a glandular surface layer of the Scutellum whose function is to digest and absorb food material stored in the endosperm

Area of Embryo: Coleoptile (protecte sheath)

Plumule (first shoot)

Adventitious root

(The Endosperm, when toasted and rolled, becomes our well-known cereal – cornflakes !)

Radicle (first root)

Coleorhiza (root she

A rough scar of attachment to the corn cob

Figure 5:   A Maize grain (monocotyledon) in L.S. (longitudinal section)

SEED VIABILITY

When the seed is fully ripened it has close to 100% germination capacity, but over time its capability for growth diminishes. Its 'viability' declines. Furthermore, the capability for the emergence of the radicle is not quite what the grower wants from seed germination – what the grower wants are leaves and a proper seedling! Old seeds may be viable botanically, but produce a less than brilliant crop due to the poorer, slow start and, maybe, sluggish growth thereafter.

Some seeds remain viable much longer than others do. For example, willow seeds are viable for only a short period (approximately 48 hours), whereas other seeds, if stored in suitable conditions, may remain viable for extensive periods – such as members of the Papilionaceae (Leguminosae) family and also wheat. Other examples of viability follow:

GENERA	AVERAGE VIABILITY (Years)
Bellis	6 – 7
Dianthus	5 – 10
Lotus	to 100
Malva	to 200
Primula	1 – 5
Vegetables:	
Broad bean	3
Lettuce	6
Onion	2

Table 1: Seed viability

SEED VIGOUR

Some seeds have much more vigour – partly this is due to seed size and larger seeds do tend to have more vigour. F1 hybrid seeds tend to have more natural hybrid vigour than open-pollinated seeds. Even large, new season seeds can loose their viability and vigour if they have insufficient care before sowing takes place. Old seeds tend to be less vigorous than young seeds. The storage of seeds is mentioned in Section 3.

PHYSIOLOGICAL PROCESSES

For successful germination to take place of viable, non-dormant (dormancy = a resting condition) seeds, water and oxygen must be available and the temperature must be within a certain range which varies with different genera, but in general lies between $5^{\circ}C$ and $30^{\circ}C$. (In practice, there should be freedom from poisons such as excessive CO_2, pests such as slugs and diseases such as *Alternaria* – a leaf spot associated with damping-off.)

Some seeds are naturally non-dormant (as against seeds with true dormancy like rose seeds with their woody fruit coat). Viable non-dormant seeds, for example seeds of garden annuals, will germinate when they have their essential requisites - moisture, oxygen and an adequate amount of warmth – within their germination range, which, remarkably, may range for some weeds from $0^{\circ}C$ to about $30^{\circ}C$ for other genera. (Seeds with dormancy factors require this dormancy to be broken before they will germinate.)

There can also be light or dark requirements and, from the gardener's point of view at least, an adequate resting place - i.e. a well-aerated compost to grow in. It is exceedingly difficult to speedily transplant the germinating seeds from a seed-testing filter paper where presumably they have as near perfect conditions for germination as can be arranged.

Water is essential for growth and development because it disperses the nutrients required, enabling the seedling to thrive. Water alone, however, will only sustain the young plant for a limited period. Without water the major nutrients, nitrogen, phosphate and potash, plus the other minor nutrients and trace elements, will not be taken up by the plant. Water is one of the three major essentials for life, the other two being air (for oxygen and carbon) and sunlight.

WATER UPTAKE

The seedcoat of many seeds acts like a piece of blotting paper – and the first water to enter the seedcoat does this by **imbibition** – a non-energy-requiring absorption of water. This, in conjunction with the oxygen in the air, enables some of the sugars (foodstuff) which are soluble, to be available and with the soluble plant hormones present, the germination process begins. More water is then absorbed by **osmosis**. Cell division and thus multiplication takes place and growth is underway.

IMBIBITION

Imbibition, the first stage in the germination process, is determined by:

a) seed composition

b) permeability of the fruit or seedcoat

c) availability of water in the environment

There are three phases in imbibition:

Phase I

Imbibition is independent of metabolic activity. It is a physical process and can occur in live and dead seeds.

Phase II

This is the period of active metabolism in live seed. (If the seeds are dead then they remain inert during this phase.) It is possible in this phase to dry the seed to re-use it at a later date without damaging the seed. It can be used as a method of synchronising germination (known as 'priming').

Phase III

This phase is associated with germination itself, with the start of mobilisation of the food reserves.

The imbibition phases can been seen when looked at as an increase in percentage of weight against time:

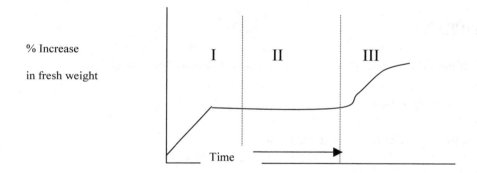

During the third phase cell division and elongation take place and the food reserves are mobilised. Enzymes are activated and food that has been stored in an insoluble form in the cotyledons or endosperm is changed into a soluble form and these sugars pass to the embryo where cell differentiation and growth of the plumule and radicle occur.

PLANT CELLS

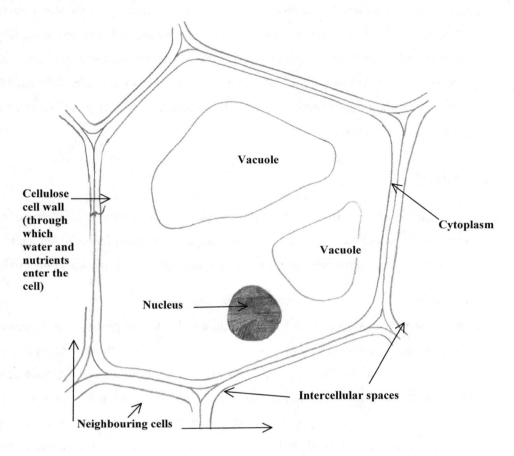

(This cell diagram shows two large vacuoles)

Figure 6: A simplified plant cell

Plant cells are complex and the cell's contents, including the sap, have some remarkable organelles, including:

Desmotubules	Endoplastic reticulum	Mitochondria
Chloroplasts	Dictyosomes	Nuclear pores
Heterochromatin	Nucleolus	Granae
Starch	Dictyosome vesicles	Coated vesicles
Ribosomes	Proteinaceous microtubule	

and the nucleus with its chromosomes and genetic code is even now only just in the realm of understanding.

The journey into the plant by water from the soil through the root system and up to a plant's leaves is achieved by a process called osmosis. In doing so the water moves to dilute the cells of the plant solutions. Water entering the cell is stored in the large central vacuole, which then expands to press the cytoplasm against a rigid cell wall. When nearly almost fully inflated the uptake of water is slowed. The cells become turgid – this inflation pressure is called turgor pressure. (For the general structure of a plant cell see Figure 6.)

OSMOSIS

The definition of osmosis is when a solution is separated by a semi-permeable membrane from its pure solvent, or from a more dilute solution, the solvent tends to pass from the more dilute solution, through the membrane and into the concentrated solution.

(It is not very clear why osmosis should occur, or what the properties are that make a membrane semi-permeable. One theory supposes that the membrane acts as a molecular sieve, having tiny pores in it that are too small to allow large molecules like sugar to pass through, but large enough to let the small water molecules go through. Another theory suggests that the solvent actually dissolves in the membrane and seeps through it by diffusion, while the solute molecules cannot dissolve in the membrane.)

[Our author's note above is included for interest rather than for the examination, HCC]

The vacuole in a plant cell contains a solution of salts and sugars. The inner cytoplasmic boundary of the vacuole, the tonoplast, is semi-permeable, while the cellulose wall is freely permeable to water and many dissolved substances. The vacuole solution exerts an osmotic pressure (a suction) and water is taken in through the cell wall and the cytoplasm. This extra water will tend to increase the volume of the vacuole, pushing the cytoplasm outward against the cell wall. In a fully-grown cell the cell wall is not extensible and does not allow the vacuole to increase in volume. The extra water taken in can only increase the pressure in it.

Uptake of water will continue until the pressure of the vacuole outwards is equal to the resistance of the cell wall inwards. The cell is then fully turgid.

The complexity of the cell is such that a conscious or unconscious sympathy with its needs is desirable in order to be a truly competent plant propagator. The plant cell is very sensitive to its supplies of oxygen, water and nutrients, and including the sugars (from the endosperm and later the work of the chloroplasts in the leaf cells in light during photosynthesis) and the hormones derived from its meristems (the regions of cell division).

RESPIRATION

Respiration in living organisms is the series of chemical changes that release energy from food material. It involves a complicated chain of chemical breakdowns accelerated by enzymes, but it can be regarded as the oxidation of carbohydrates to form carbon dioxide and water, with a corresponding release of energy. This is broadly similar to our respiration where our bodies break down foodstuffs which are "oxidised" to release energy for our use. We also breathe out carbon dioxide and water as vapour.

Aerobic Respiration

Sometimes this process is called cellular or tissue respiration, or internal respiration, to distinguish it from the breathing-in of oxygen, which is also misleadingly called "respiration". The energy released by respiration is used for such activities as growth, development and the secretion of enzymes. It can be regarded as one of the most important aspects of the vital chemistry of living matter. For respiration to occur sugars and oxygen must be taken in and to react together. Carbon dioxide and water, which are the end products of the reaction, must constantly be removed or the cells will die.

Anaerobic Respiration

Should the seedbed become waterlogged, or alternatively "capped", the seeds may suffer from waterlogging – a sort of death by drowning – or from the capped seedbed. A carbon dioxide narcosis may occur which, again, may prevent seed germination. Dead seeds may ferment - a form of anaerobic respiration.

Anaerobic respiration is unlikely to occur in seedbeds that have been prepared in a reasonable way. The organisms that bring about this form of respiration can themselves live in the absence of atmospheric oxygen. They do this by chemically reducing the source of oxygen in the soil particles and organic material around them. Sometimes soils dug up from land that lies wet may look blue in colour and smell of bad eggs. These are indicators of sulphides in place of the sulphates and of hydrogen sulphide gas, produced by the anaerobic decay of organic matter and the chemical reduction of the soil particles brought about by anaerobic bacteria.

SEED DORMANCY

If a viable (fertile) seed is subjected to favourable environmental conditions it will germinate; if it fails to do so then the seed is said to be dormant. Dormant seeds will germinate once certain pre-determined factors have been fulfilled **and** provided the necessary environmental conditions (i.e. moisture, oxygen and warmth) are appropriate. Dormancy can be seen as a natural defence mechanism to prevent germination occurring during or just before adverse climatic conditions, e.g. cold weather or periods of low rainfall. During dormancy, respiration occurs at a very low rate, but there is little other metabolic activity or growth.

Some seeds are easy to germinate (mustard and cress, for example) but others are very difficult and this is usually due to such seeds exhibiting a state of dormancy. This frequently occurs in trees and shrubs (and is therefore a challenge for growers) but is found less often in food crops.

Various forms of dormancy have been classified:

1. Seedcoat dormancy – the dormancy caused by embryo coverings
2. Immature embryo dormancy
3. Cold temperature dormancy
4. Epicotyl dormancy
5. Germination inhibitors or growth promoters

Some plants occur in more than one group, e.g. *Fraxinus excelsior* (ash) which displays immature embryo dormancy, cold temperature dormancy and, on many occasions, seedcoat dormancy. *Tilia* (lime) and *Carpinus* (hornbeam) also develop hard seed coats and require a period of cold to break cold dormancy. These plants are then said to have multiple dormancy factors.

Seedcoat (testa) Dormancy

This is either due to a hard seedcoat and/or a water impermeable coat.

Hard seedcoat: a hard seedcoat can cause physical limitations to the growth of the embryo. It limits water uptake and limits the diffusion of oxygen. Naturally, the seedcoat is gradually broken down by environmental factors, a process that can take an undetermined length of time and result in very erratic germination. It occurs most speedily given warm, moist conditions. A grower can speed up this process and obtain a more satisfactory germination percentage by mechanical **scarification** - rubbing the seed with abrasive grit, or rolling between sheets of emery paper.

Chipping may be used to break through the hard seedcoat if seed is large enough to handle and the edge of a file is relatively easy and safe to use. Alternatively, the **acid bath** method is the most reliable and accurate, but much skill and very safe procedures are needed particularly when handling acids. The seeds are soaked in a strong acid solution to weaken the coat (sulphuric acid 90% or nitric acid) at a temperature of 18-20°C for a specific amount of time – minutes only - that has been determined by a pilot study. The seeds go very black and may heat up – it is a process requiring considerable care.

Epicotyl Dormancy

This is a rare form of dormancy, which can be broken/removed by low temperatures. With these seeds when germination occurs the radicle (young root) emerges from the testa (seed coat) and begins to grow, but the epicotyl (young stem of the embryo and seedling above the cotyledons) will not grow until the seed has undergone a period of stratification. The seed requires the warmth of the first summer for the root to develop, but the cold of the second winter for the dormancy to break the epicotyl dormancy to allow the shoot to grow away during the second spring or summer.

Examples of this 'two season' type of dormancy can be seen in some species of lily, such as *Lilium auratum*, also in *Paeonia suffruticosa* (the tree paeony*), Viburnum opulus* (Wayfaring tree), *Smilax* species, *Davidia* (the handkerchief tree) and in *Chionanthus*, the latter three being genera from the North American continent.

It can be seen that the development of an impermeable testa can be advantageous for survival in some climatic conditions as the seeds may survive prolonged droughts.

DORMANCY IN BROAD-LEAVED TREE SEEDS

It is known that some seeds contain a chemical inhibitor, coupled with an endosperm barrier, which stops gaseous exchange and, therefore, germination.

While delayed or irregular germination may be beneficial for reproduction in the wild, its occurrence in the nursery can be a problem to the grower. This is because it leads to stock of different ages and sizes, makes it harder to collect a uniform batch of plants for an order dispatch, ties up bed space for longer than normal and generally increases production costs.

The grower requires an even and uniform crop of seedlings in the first year, so most broad-leaved tree seeds are treated in some way prior to sowing to overcome dormancy and promote rapid germination.

Because of the diversity of dormancy combinations, every species should be treated in a specific manner to remove the dormancy. These treatments are usually based on the natural conditions that would be experienced by the seeds and which offer the most effective methods of breaking dormancy. These may be deduced by studying the natural history of a species' seed between dispersal and subsequent germination.

A tribute to Mr. Mansfield – Roadman.

In the hot summer of 1944, he showed me the effect a bonfire on the germination of dormant grass and weed seeds. It was Mr. Mansfield's 65th birthday and he was to retire very shortly but he took the trouble to tell and show me (a very small boy) that where he had burnt some weeds on the meadow beside the road, the bare ground where the fire had been would be full of sprouting grasses and weed seedlings after the first rain. This happened as he described it, but I never made use of this data!

This effect on the germination of dormant seeds is now described scientifically and the gases involved – notably ethylene – identified. The technique of smoking seeds is particularly useful for some South African and Australian species which are exposed to fire in their native habitat.

It is relatively easy to make some smoke by burning dry hay, straw or bracken. On a small scale a bee-keeper's smoker provides a controlled facility. Set out the sown, soaked seeds in their pots pans or trays in a large box fairly well closed in and smoke for about ½ an hour. Time enough for the smoke to enter the compost. It is also possible to water on the ash from such fires. Kits can be bought which have the essence of the smoke and ash from burning the wild flowers and straw from the South African veldt. (Karen Platt in her book 'Growing from Seed' reports that the hairs on the protea seeds need to be burnt off before the seeds will germinate.)

(A warning – my first effort of using smoke was to break the dormancy of Freesia corms raised from seed. These I smoked in a covered wheelbarrow. I used straw and it started gently enough but the fire needed air and it became a firey affair when the straw lit up well in the polytunnel! - The treatment worked!)

2. THE IMPORTANCE OF SEED TREATMENTS

Treatments to seeds between seed harvest and sowing are applied for one or more reasons:

(1) Convenience of handling, sowing, economic use.

(2) Health of seed and disease prevention.

(3) Physiological reasons, such as dormancy breaking.

(4) Legislation – to meet the requirements of the 1920 Seeds Act and subsequent revisions.

(1)   **Convenience Treatments**

(a)   Seeds are pre-sown in suitable media (amateur use).

(b)   Taped seeds (enables seeding at pre-determined spacing). The tape takes up moisture and decays. (Amateur use – this is sometimes used for lawn grass.)

(c)   Pelleted seeds (the most generally used method used at present). The seed is covered in successive layers of inert substance, such as clay mineral. This can make their size and shape uniform, which eases their use for precision sowing and mechanised drilling.

(d)   Split pills - these enable the seed to get more oxygen. One of the snags of the clay pellet is that it swells with water on contact with moist media (soil) and this may exclude further supplies of air.

(e)   Fruit clusters, like the seeds of beet, may be rubbed to lower the number of seedlings, which could emerge from one apparent seed.

Pelleted Seed

The use and development of precision drills has allowed crops to be sown in straight rows with easier inter-row cultivation for weed control and eliminating the need for the use of labour later on for singling the individual plants.

The various machines use either belts with holes in them, discs with holes, or revolving cups. They are designed to pick up seeds one at a time and place them in the ground at a pre-determined spacing and depth.

Seed and multi-plug trays are sometimes space-sown using a vacuum technique – to pick up a single seed – sucked onto the end of a fine tube.

Drills are adapted by changing the belts or discs to accept different sized seeds. Difficulty arises when the seeds are not round, but elongated, pointed, or flat, such as lettuce, carrot, and turnips - such types cannot be picked up easily by a precision drill.

This problem is overcome in precision sowing by coating the seed with a layer of inert material in such a way that it is as near spherical as possible and can be easily picked up by the drill mechanism. In some processes the material used for coating is such that it reacts hygroscopically in contact with the soil moisture, swells and splits within minutes, thus allowing emergence of the radicle and plumule.

Other materials can be added to the coating substance, such as fungicides to prevent damping-off disease, and nutrients and growth-stimulating substances.

The Advantages of Pelleted Seeds are:

- Small and expensive seed can be sown without the need for pricking or singling out later.
- Sturdier plants from less dense sowings, overcoming seedling competition at the earliest stages.
- The high value of many seeds, especially F1 hybrids, requires economy in seed material.
- Possibilities of adding certain active constituents, such as fungicides, insecticides, nutrients and water conductive colloids to hasten germination.

VEGETABLE SEEDS FOR PRECISION DRILLING		
CROP	NATURAL SEEDS SHAPE	SEED WHEN PREPARED FOR PRECISION DRILLING
CARROT		
PARSNIP		
LETTUCE		
RADISH		*
ONION		
CELERY		
LEEK		
BEET		*
BRASSICA		

* Beet seed and radish are graded rather than pelleted

Table 2: Vegetable seeds for precision drilling

(2)   Treatments for Seed Health and Disease Prevention

The use of pesticide treatments for the control or eradication of seed-borne diseases or pests, or to protect the seeds and the resultant seedlings from attack.

There are two groups of treatment given. The fungicide, bactericide or insecticide may be applied to the seeds as a dust, slurry, or as a constituent of the coating of the pellet to surround the seed as a pelleted seed.

The other form of treatment is given without trace, such as fumigation of onion seed against seed-borne stem and bulb eelworm with Methyl-bromide. Seed surface sterilisation with aerated steam, or Thiram soaking against seed-borne fungus diseases. (NB: Methyl-bromide gas is exceedingly toxic and this type of treatment would only be used by the seed company.)

The eradication of the few seed-borne bacterial diseases is especially difficult, but some antibiotics such as streptomycin or Kasugamycin have been used at research stations for controlling Halo Blight on *Phaseolus* (runner beans).

Virus diseases can also be transmitted via seeds and one virus-infected seed plus one parthenogenetic aphid to act as the vector can cause loss to a whole area of crop in a field of lettuce. The answer to this at present is inspection at seed source. Lettuce seed lots sold as 'Mosaic-tested' contain less than one infected seed in a thousand. Where the risk of seed-borne Tomato Mosaic virus is present, the seed can be cleaned up either by dry heat treatment, or by trisodium phosphate.

Most seed crops are grown and bulked up in hot dry regions where:
(a) the risk of disease is minimal
(b) the conditions for crop growth are excellent
(c) there are few sources of genetic contamination from similar crop species in the area
(d) the conditions for the harvest of seed are excellent

There are other risks involved in seed raising away from the regions where the crop will be grown:

a. the seeds are not acclimatised to our requirements
b. the crop is not surveyed and rogued for diseases to the same level of efficiency
c. the essential 'true-to-type' characteristics may be diluted by varietal abnormalities not adequately removed (rogued) prior to the seed harvest.

Control of Seed-borne Diseases

- The Thiram soak treatment of carrot, celery and pea seeds is effective in controlling fungal diseases such as *Septoria* and black rot. The seed is treated in 80% Thiram powder solution at 30°C for 24 hours. Dry after treatment.

- Hot water treatment is used for canker disease in broccoli and diseases in celery seed. This is done by dipping the seed in hot water at 50°C for 25 minutes.

- Heat treatment is used for cleaning cucumber seed for Cucumber Green-mottle-virus. With treatment in a hot air oven for 3 days at 70°C. Tomato can be treated in the same way for Tomato Mosaic virus for 4 days at 70° C.

(3)   Physiological Reasons

Seed treatments for breaking dormancy are:
- Mechanical scarification – by chipping, puncturing, abrasive acid treatment.
- Gibberellic acid treatment at not more than 100mg per litre of water is widely used to soak the seeds to break down the testa. Ethephon is sometimes used, which releases the gaseous hormone ethylene.
- Thermal treatments – dormancy is controlled by a high or lower temperature limit.
- Hormone treatment can be used to raise the 'temperature ceiling'.

Example = Lettuce seed, according to variety, does not germinate at temperatures higher than about 27–30°C, but will do so after a 15 minute soak in a solution of kinetin (10mg per litre of water) in full light conditions. (In practical terms the growers of lettuce plants would put their own trays of seed into the cold store for a couple of days, whereafter the seeds germinate at 15°C normally.)

Celery seed which will not germinate above 21°C unless they have received a special treatment of a mixture of gibberellins and cytokinin. Cyclamen, freesia and polyanthus seed can require similar treatment.

- Stratification - deep dormancy found in many Rosaceae is broken by stratification. Several months at 2-7°C. This can be shortened by preceding the cold treatment by a 'warm' period of four weeks at 25°C. This matures the embryo to a stage ready for germination.
  Pure nitrogen atmosphere, at any temperature, can sometimes be substituted for low temperature treatment by stratification.

STRATIFICATION

This is a 'moist, low temperature treatment of seed' which overcomes embryo dormancy in many perennial plants, shrubs and some trees. The need for this treatment over a period would in nature ensure that seeds in temperate regions do not germinate until the passing of winter and the renewal of favourable conditions for successful growth of the young plant.

In horticulture, seeds are stratified by holding them over the winter period outside in trays of moist sand, peat or vermiculite or, in some cases in a refrigerator, for 10 to 20 weeks at about 5°C. (See Figure 7).

The medium must hold sufficient water for the germinating seed, but not so much as to inhibit oxygen availability and gaseous exchange to take place.

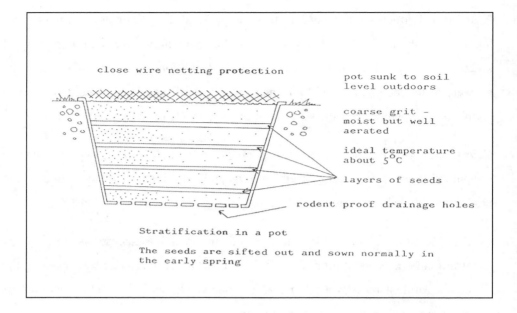

Figure 7: Diagram of Stratification pit

VERNALISATION

Low temperatures encountered by imbibed seeds can also promote flowering of some species, particularly winter annuals. This effect was first exploited by Lysenko (1898-1976), a Soviet biologist and agronomist, who thought that the genetic make-up of the plants was altered by low temperatures. [NB: Lysenko's doctrines and claims have largely been discredited but his influence as the total autocrat for Soviet biology in Stalin's era was not without some success.]

Vernalisation is the promotion of flower initiation by a previous cold treatment. In most species that can be vernalised the seed must have developed into young plants, i.e. germinated, before they respond to cold.

The vernalisation treatment for winter wheat enables this seed to be sown in the spring. This has huge advantages where the soil conditions in the autumn have meant sowing has not been possible.

CHEMICAL STIMULANTS TO BREAK DORMANCY
AND IMPROVE GROWTH

Pre-soaking in solutions of some chemicals can improve the performance of seeds. Soaking cotton seed in boric acid meets the high boron requirement of this crop. A treatment similar in many respects is **drought-hardening** - but this involves soaking the seeds in potassium nitrate solution, accelerating the early growth of outdoor tomatoes and improves the profitability of the crop in a climate where the short period suitable for growth limits yield.

The inhibition of growth due to seed dormancy can be overcome by **environmental manipulation** - soaking the seed in a solution of a growth-promoting substance. For example, soaking lettuce seed in a kinetin solution has ensured that high temperature- induced dormancy does not affect germination in the field.

Growth substances can sometimes be safely introduced to the seed by soaking them in solutions mixed in organic solvents such as acetone or dichloromethane for 24 to 48 hours and then allowing the solvents to evaporate off immediately.

Breaking of dormancy is frequently associated with the disappearance of inhibitors in the seed, rather than the appearance of a growth promoter. Gibberellic acid often plays a part in stimulating shoot growth once dormancy is broken, but it appears that this hormone can itself break the dormancy of some species. This applies particularly to woody species such as Horse Chestnut (*Aesculus hippocastanum*), Beech (*Fagus sylvatica*), and rhododendron species.

Kinetin causes bud-break in some species like Apple (*Malus vulgaris*). A solution of ethylene chlorohydrin will also break dormancy of the buds of many woody species. The use of these chemicals for forcing early blooms of Lilac (*Syringa vulgaris*) or breaking the dormancy of Lily-of-the-Valley (*Convallaria majalis*) rhizomes is now well established.

(In the normal way Lily-of-the-Valley requires 6 weeks of winter temperature before it will develop a flowering stem. This is a very short period for the production of a forced flower crop between lifting – say in early October for cold store conditions prior to planting in late November. This provides the chilling requirement for flowers in the pre-Christmas period. Specialist growers of AYR (all year round) 'Valley' keep the dormant crowns in cold store from lifting and for 12-15 months prior to forcing the number of 'pips' they require to meet specific orders or targets. The crop flowers in about 21 days.)

Corms of some Gladiolus cultivars can be successfully forced within a week of lifting - provided they are treated for 3 or 4 days with ethylene chlorhydrin at the rate of 4ml of 40 per cent solution per litre of corms.

Water is also a potent breaker of dormancy in some species. Dormant onion bulbs will begin to produce adventitious roots if they are wetted for 48 to 72 hours. Thus, if it rains during the ripening of the crop in the field, bulbs are produced with a much-reduced dormancy and sprouting in store becomes a serious problem. This happens even if the bulbs are subsequently dried and the roots shrivelled.

Immersion in hot water (30°C) for 10 to 12 hours, or 40°C to 55°C for 15 seconds is used commercially to break the dormancy of lilac and *Forsythia* flower buds. In this instance the correct temperature to the water is vital.

SEED PRIMING

Seed priming is a pre-sowing treatment which improves the establishment of the resulting seedlings by speeding germination and making this more uniform, with the result that all seeds germinate together by bringing them to the same stage of development before sowing.

When a batch of seeds is dried for storage, their (after-ripening) development stops at different times so that each seed is in a different stage of germination potential. When the seeds are sown, and absorb water, the different stages are noticeable.

Priming the seeds brings them all to a stage of readiness at the same time and then holds them, just as the radicle is about to emerge. To do this, the seeds absorb just enough water to get to this stage. By preventing more water entering, development is stopped.

Allowing the seeds to imbibe in a strong solution of a non-toxic chemical has this useful controlling effect. The osmotic strength of the solution in the seed, at the point just before germination, is balanced by the concentration outside. This stops the inward water flow, which halts development. Primed seeds do not stay viable for long.

The effect of priming and that of cold stratification are similar. Priming blocks seed development by controlling the amount of water entering the seed, while some researchers believe that stratification allows seeds to develop to a point. Further development needs higher temperatures.

For seed priming it is important to choose a chemical which is not toxic. Most of the experimental work has been carried out using a chemical similar to motor car antifreeze, called polyethene glycol (PEG). In practice the right strength is found by experimenting with a range of concentrations.

CHITTING OF SEEDS

The 'chitting' of seeds is done by allowing them to take up water from a moist, but airy, medium until their radicles just begin to protrude. Small seeds can be mixed with a suitable carrier material and then sown in suitable soil. This `chitting' method shortens the time from sowing to seedling emergence.

The National Vegetable Research Station originally developed a `Fluid Drill' which extruded chitted seeds mixed into a colloidal fluid of alginate. This became commercial and was very successful, but it did require more management skills and reliable weather conditions – not always easy to guarantee 48 hours in advance.

Success of the system depends on not allowing the seeds to dry out during the process and preventing injury to the seed radicles. A variation of this system has been used for the direct drilling of trees and shrubs on site, especially on motorway embankments and verges.

In essence fluid drilling has been around for about a century or more – a wallpaper paste-like fluid (of gravy-like consistency) can carry the seeds without the seeds settling to the bottom, provided there is some gentle agitation. The fluid can be directed into the seed drill and this will space out the seeds well depending on the rate of flow of the seeds in the 'syrup' and the rate of travel of the drill.

The huge step forward was the use of the chitted seeds. The young radicle emerging maybe 5mm is very fragile, but the syrupy fluid handles the seed very kindly. The seeds once in the seedbed are able to grow away very speedily, aiding their establishment and ability to compete with weeds, pests and diseases.

The chitting of the seeds can be achieved in an aerated tank of water, or by immersion of the 'sack of seeds' and then spin-drying. This would be repeated on a 6-12 hourly basis until the seeds started to chit. The difficulty with the system is the question of how to hold the chitted seeds, for some days if necessary, to accommodate weather problems and the difficulty of drilling in wet soil.

(4)   Seed Legislation

[NB: Although this topic is not included in the syllabus, I feel it is relevant to the plant propagation theme and important data for the Advanced student to be acquainted with at this level - OM.]

The Seeds Act of 1920 set out important standards for purity and germination capacity for a range of common agricultural seeds. Up to this date it was possible to sell seeds which were old or damaged, dead or contaminated with dirt or weed seeds. Some injurious seeds were to be excluded completely and this has eliminated a now rare weed from our fields – the fully parasitic Common Dodder (*Cuscuta epithymum*).

The production and sale of seed in this country is controlled by regulations to be found in MAFF's 'Guide to the Seeds Regulations' [visit MAFF's website on the Internet – www.maff.gov.uk which gives some information]. These rules are laid down by the European Community and include:

(a) **field inspection** – the crop is examined in the field to make sure it is true to variety, in good health and that precautions have been taken to prevent cross pollination.

(b) **sampling** – samples are taken for testing, other than standard seeds of vegetables or uncertified pre-basic seeds.

(c) **testing** – laboratory testing is done to ensure that the seed complies with the statutory regulations. (This includes a minimum rate of germination.)

COLLECTION AND CLEANING OF SEED

A large number of specialist growers of woody plants collect their own seed because it is relatively unobtainable and provenance (see Section 6) is "all" when it comes to the quality of the plants themselves. Seed should be collected from the parent plant at the correct level of maturity. If collected too early the embryo will not be sufficiently developed and if too late then dispersal will probably have taken place. Those plants with dry seeds and fruit can be collected and dried for a few weeks before separation of the seed from the fruit by some mechanical method (e.g. threshing). Further cleaning to remove chaff, etc. is done by screens, air blowers, etc.

Plants that produce indehiscent fruit, such as grasses and cereals, can be cut and threshed in one operation. The seed is often quite difficult to remove and any damage will result in reduced viability. Usually the seed needs to be dried after harvesting under controlled conditions.

Fleshy fruits such as tomato, cucumbers, etc. have the seed removed, cleaned and dried. Commercially the fruit can be macerated and the pulp and seed are separated by a process of fermentation.

Conifer seed is extracted by leaving the cones to dry naturally for a few weeks so that they will open, or by artificially drying them for a few hours.

A method of flotation is often used for fleshy and aggregate fruits.

SEED TESTING AND VIABILITY

Good quality seed is genetically true to species or cultivar, has a high germination rate, is free from disease and pests and has a high percentage of '**purity**' – i.e. is free from weed seeds, other crop seeds and any other extraneous matter. Purity is the percentage by weight of the 'pure seed' in a sample. It is determined by a visual examination of individual seed in a weighed sample.

The purpose of testing for viability is to determine the germination percentage, which could be useful if you should have a large stock of a previous year's seeds in store. To make an accurate test 400 seeds should be taken at random from the batch and divided into groups of 100. The sample is first visually inspected. They are then tested with a scalpel or x-ray to ascertain if the embryo is present. If more than 10% are empty then they are re-cleaned and a sample sown for the viability test. This initial sowing takes place in light and at a constant temperature of 21°C. If the germination rate is greater than 75% then the seeds are considered viable and the rest of the batch are returned to store until time for distribution. If less than 75% germination occurs then the seeds are transferred to fluctuating temperatures. From this sector if more than 75% germinate then the rest of the batch are returned to store. If less than 75% germinate then a **tetrazolium test** (a biochemical method of testing for viability by soaking the seed in a light-sensitive salt) is carried out and if the seeds fail this then they are considered to have failed the test.

As an alternative to the foregoing process, the seeds may be tested for various forms of dormancy (e.g. chipped, chilled, after-ripening and plant growth regulators). If after dormancy testing germination is more than 75% then the seed is retained. If less than 75% then the seed is either discarded or passed on for further research.

3. ENVIRONMENTAL FACTORS AFFECTING THE GERMINATION OF SEEDS

There are four environmental factors that will favour the germination of seeds: water, oxygen, temperature and light. Unfavourable factors in the environment can be the excessive presence of poisons – residual herbicides, excessive fertilizers, other chemicals like boron, unfavourable gases – SO_2 and, to excess, CO_2 - and volatile hormones like the ester forms of 24D.

The total environment surrounding the seed may also hold biological problems for the seeds. Freedom from competition – the main groups of competitors include:

1. Pests like the flea beetle or slugs
2. Diseases - such as the group of diseases generally called "damping off", e.g. *Pythium*
3. Weeds
4. Excessive competition from the crop itself due to sowing too thickly

WATER

Seeds need water to germinate but they also need air - so the seeds must not have water to the exclusion of air. The ideal seedbed is moist and this moisture is held on the surface of the soil particles, within the aggregates and within the colloidal particles. The surplus water has to be able to drain away leaving air spaces. The classical description of a firm, fine seedbed provides the small seeds close contact with the water films and the air spaces. Water films tend to spread and in this way the seed absorbs its water by imbibition.

The ideal situation in the field is to irrigate, if need be to field capacity, a day or two before the final seedbed preparation. Then later on, when the soil is no longer sticky, the seedbed can be prepared.

If one has to water after sowing there is a risk that the surface particles may cap – run together to make a sealed surface layer. This can exclude supplies of oxygen and the natural build up of CO_2 in the living soil may reduce germination. Also the soil cap or crust on the surface may mechanically prevent germination.

Mist, as a system of irrigation, does little damage to soil structure but it is difficult to use outside because the water tends to blow away. Overhead irrigation with large heavy droplets of water in particular may weaken the gums which hold soil crumbs together and so let the soil particles silt together to cap the compost, cut off the oxygen supply and reduce the opportunity for germination.

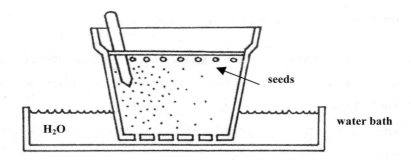

seeds

H₂O

water bath

Figure 8:   A first watering system

A useful technique for the first watering of seeds in containers is to stand the pot or tray of sown seeds in a shallow water bath and to let the moisture rise up through the compost until it glistens on the surface (see Figure 8). Remove the pot, drain and place in the propagator to await germination. This system tends not to dislodge the seeds, as can happen when using a fine rose, and furthermore the structure quality of the seed compost is retained. Heavy overhead sprays may weaken the gums that hold soil crumbs together and so let the soil particles silt together to cap the compost.

Good drainage is an essential feature of successful and vigorous seedling production. All field drainage systems must be very satisfactory if adequate aeration of soil is to be maintained. In effect surplus water must be able to drain below the root zone to a water table not closer than c.600mm from the soil surface.

OXYGEN

Seeds need oxygen for respiration. When germination begins, the respiration rate speeds up and the free exchange of air around the seed becomes very important.

This **aeration** is obtained in many seed composts by the addition of granulated peat and coarse sand. In the outdoor seedbed, aeration is obtained by the creation of a good crumb structure. Lack of oxygen is caused by a waterlogged seedbed, or by a capping of the media surface due to heavy rain, irrigation or unnecessary mechanical compaction or trampling of the soil when wet.

TEMPERATURE

Temperature requirements vary greatly for different kinds of seed. In controlled conditions under glass, seeds can be supplied with the ideal germinating temperature. The temperature should be measured exactly where the seed is – rather than in the space within the glasshouse or propagator (see Figure 9). These temperatures are of value of course, but the seeds themselves may be located several degrees C higher or lower than the target optimum temperature. The covering of glass and paper or polythene will help to maintain the temperature in a seed tray (but this too has its hazards with an increase in the relative humidity and the chances for some damping-off fungi to flourish).

Figure 9: To measure the temperature where the seeds are germinating

When attempting to encourage as long and as effective a growing season as possible, the most obvious factor within the environment that will promote plant growth is the warmth of the growing site. If the site is in such a position that the average ambient temperatures will be higher than surrounding areas, it will provide a condition for earlier and more rapid germination, faster seedling growth and a longer growing season. A southerly aspect will encourage an earlier increase in soil temperature in the spring and higher temperatures throughout the season.

However, the soil temperature is not only an effect of aspect but will also be governed by the soil type. Heavy clay and silty soils tend to be slower to warm up than more open, coarse, sandy soils that hold less water. The soil temperature will also be governed by shelter and the incidence of radiation frost – thus demonstrating that environmental factors cannot be considered in isolation.

Frost Incidence

If, by satisfactory siting, the growing season is advanced to induce earlier germination and seedling emergence, the seedlings may be at risk over longer periods to the incidence of radiation frost. Considerations related to the choice of site must therefore initially assess the incidence of such frosts in the area in terms of probable risk. The risk should be assessed in terms of the local topography and the site should allow for adequate cold air drainage so that the actual occurrence of ground and air frost over the seedbed is reduced to a minimum. Attention should also be given to the provision made for shelter, so that cold air drainage is not artificially impeded, e.g. by hedges and other windbreaks.

Shelter

The effect of wind speed is usually the most under-estimated environmental aspect in the establishment of the seedbed. The effect of wind on seedling growth by causing physical damage to leaves, water loss from the plant and temperature reduction is very often completely overlooked. Exposure to even apparently low wind speeds (e.g. above 0.5 mph), such as occur in summer, influences the rate of seedling growth.

LIGHT

Most seeds will germinate in light or darkness. However, some need light for germination; others germinate much better in the absence of light.

The recommendation is to site the growing area with a southerly aspect with its increased temperature; also the site will have good light levels unless the shelter causes much obscuring of incoming radiation.

The importance of light is necessary in relation to the promotion of photosynthesis and the provision, in consequence, of adequate carbohydrates for active growth.

Phytochrome

Quoting from the new RHS Dictionary of Gardening: "there is good evidence that the light-sensitive pigment phytochrome may play a pivotal role in the control of seed germination".

Phytochrome is a remarkable protein that is stable and exists in two forms, active and inactive, which are reversible. The inactive form absorbs red light and is called P_R. The active form P_{FR} absorbs far-red light. Light converts each to the other form. Red light (660nm wavelength) converts P_R to P_{FR} and far-red (730nm) light converts P_{FR} to P_R.

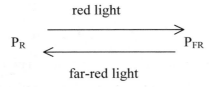

Each form of light reverses the state of the phytochrome.

Natural daylight has both red and far-red radiation in a balance, but under a leafy canopy in a forest this balance is altered and with the loss of much of the red radiation, the germination of many seeds is inhibited. The same applies to light-sensitive seeds sown too deeply in the soil.

Examples of seeds requiring light include:
- *Lamium purpureum* - 'red dead nettle'
- Lettuce – germination is strongly promoted by red light
- *Arabidopsis thaliana*
- *Sinapsis arvensis* - 'charlock'
- Primrose

Well-known examples include: *Antirrhinum, Alyssum, Begonia, Impatiens, Mimulus, Nicotiana, Petunia* and *Polyanthus*

Seeds whose germination may be inhibited by light include:

- Tomato
- Lettuce – germination of some cultivars may be inhibited by far-red light.

Etiolation

In the absence of light the young seedlings epicotyl shoot develops rapidly, growing upwards towards the light - a **phototropic** response. On reaching daylight its development slows and real growth takes place with the differentiation of the new cells to become the leaves (which turn green) and indeed the new plant. If there is insufficient light the seedlings will continue to grow from the germinated seed and the shoot will become etiolated - blanched (due to lack of chlorophyll) and leggy. These drawn seedlings are very difficult to handle.

SPECIAL TREATMENTS

To encourage some seeds to germinate special treatments may be necessary. Delayed germination may be caused by hard seedcoats. This may be overcome by various treatments such as abrasion, treatment with acid or alkali, soaking in water, treatment with boiling water or flame and alternate freezing and thawing. (A useful reference to such methods is to be found in *Seed Dormancy and Germination* by J W Bradbeer.)

Of a more practical nature, the RHS Members' Wisley Seed List (distributed to members of the RHS) has a genus list with seed germination requirements including:

Sown in Autumn	*Adonis*
Chill if no seedlings appear in 3 months	*Adonis*
Pre-chill sow in Spring	*Androsace*
Pre-soak	*Alstroemeria*
Seeds take 30 to 90 days to germinate	*Actaea*
Seeds take more than 90 days	*Betula*
Leave seeds uncovered when sown	*Allium*

Barely cover seeds	*Anemone*
May need two chilling periods to break dormancy	*Alnus*
Keep moist and dark	*Cyclamen*
Use lime-free compost	*Erica*
May take over a year to germinate	*Acer*
Chilling may improve germination	*Chaenomeles*
May take two winters to germinate	*Euonymus*
Sow shallowly	*Colchicum*
Sow outside	*Colchicum*
Hot water treatment – pour boiling water over the seed to promote germination	*Glycyrrhiza* (also Parsley)
Cold stratify the seed	*Rosa* sp. / alpines
Place in the coldest part of the fridge	*Rosa* sp. / alpines
Length of time in weeks (4 weeks)	*Leucojum*
Warm stratify the seed	*Ilex*
Place seed in a reasonably warm position, e.g. airing cupboard	Cactus
Length of time in weeks (4 weeks)	*Sorbus*
In the case of *Sorbus*, the warm treatment to precede a 12 week cold stratification	

Table 3: Seed germination requirements

HYGIENE AND PLANT PATHOGENS

'Damping-off' is usually due to *Phytophthora* and *Pythium* – several different species of soil and water-borne fungi may cause damping-off. Seedlings of lettuce, tomato, mustard and bedding plants are most susceptible to infection by *Pythium* and collapse at soil level. Overcrowding encourages the disease; therefore seed should be sown thinly in sterilised soil or soilless compost. The organisms that cause damping-off are often present in untreated soils; wet conditions – maybe due to the less than ideal media and over-watering can encourage the disease.

It is therefore essential to practice as much hygiene as possible in the glasshouse or any other part of the nursery/growing room.

Hygiene

The source of infection from damping-off diseases can be from the soil, the structure, any existing plants or plant material present and from soil, plants and people who enter the glasshouse environment.

In an amateur situation the problems are usually compounded by the lack of space. There are usually plants growing and composts/pots and the like stored in the greenhouse making it difficult to enable a thorough clean and so start the season empty to await the arrival of a new crop. This system of a clean start really does reduce the opportunity for infection to carry over.

In professional use, the whole structure would be thoroughly washed down with a powerful jet and ideally using hot water with a detergent – walls, glass, benching, paths – almost everywhere (but not the auto control box!). Most probably the soil media is bought in and the reliability of the supplier should ensure that it arrives free from contamination. This also applies to the containers to be used for the crop.

The opportunity for contamination from the moment these materials arrive needs careful consideration. The old potting shed floor may be the worst place because it may have the dust and debris of earlier failed crops. Where such locations have to be used, then it would be wise to consider a routine hygiene programme of disinfection drenches following a thorough clean out.

Some nurseries have a tradition of difficulty with pests and diseases and, while it may not be "their fault", it would be useful to go back to first principles and see what the sources of infection actually are and endeavour to quarantine any plants that 'must be kept' and really try to run a clean environment.

The following points are worth particular attention:

- Give as much light as possible to young seedlings without excessive heat.
- Regular use of fungicides as a preventative measure.

- The use of new, clean seed trays and pots and the regular removal of any dead leaves or rubbish anywhere in frames or under glass.

- Annual cleaning of glasshouses to help reduce infections. Similarly, cleaning away all waste after each crop is finished, before the next is commenced.

Phytophthora, a fungal infection, is always a major threat to hardy nursery stock and is often introduced with new stock plants or in water from infected sources. There are a number of suitable fungicides available for the commercial grower or private gardener, but the least costly and best remedy is to keep all growing environments as clean and tidy as possible to prevent disease in the first instance.

ENVIRONMENTAL CONSIDERATIONS OF SEED STORAGE

In order to maintain a useful degree of viability in a seed sample, some knowledge of the environmental conditions necessary for their successful storage is required. This entails an assessment of the circumstances that will enhance the length of time at which acceptable levels of viability will be maintained and involves slowing the metabolic processes within the seed which are essential to continual life but which can be reduced without detriment.

The length of a successful storage period will be a function of how much these processes can be affected and is achieved by slowing down the process of respiration in the seed, preventing the deterioration of stored food reserves and by immobilising certain essential enzymes. Storage may also be regarded as a period in which the embryo is maintained in a quiescent state and the environmental factors affecting germination are reduced to an acceptable minimum.

However, storage has a deleterious effect on the viability and quality of a seed sample over a period of time. Under normal circumstances, without any artificial storage control, a sample of seed will show the typical fall-off in viability and any storage controls merely attenuate the curve, thus maintaining viability over a longer period.

In practice, storage is achieved by decreasing the rate at which certain metabolic processes occur and this is normally done by:

a) **Reducing temperatures so that the rate of biochemical reaction is curtailed.** Normally one would expect chemical reactions to double in rate for every 10°C rise in temperature and conversely halve for every reduction of the same decrease. Most plant biochemical reactions are effectively slowed to very low levels at 5°C and any decrease in this level, although marginal, can be extremely effective. However, the affect of temperatures below 0°C are not well documented and although most seeds are known to survive freezing, in many cases it would appear to depend on the hardiness of the sample and on the speed of temperature drop. A useful temperature for the long-term storage of seed is –5°C.

b) **Reduction in the moisture content of the seed (seed drying)** is effective if it is below a level critical for the mobilisation of certain water-soluble materials and so reduces metabolic activity. However, this is complicated by levels to which desiccation can occur in particular seeds and, again, this is influenced by other considerations such as the type of stored food. Fats and oils degenerate if moisture levels are even slightly reduced.

c) **Reduction of the atmospheric moisture content** – if the seeds are kept very dry in a sealed container with desiccant silica gel the seed life is prolonged. In practical terms, when the seeds (stored, say, in a plastic, sealed, empty 2 litre ice-cream carton with a container of silica gel) are taken out of the –5°C refrigerator and the container is opened, water from the relative humidity in the air rapidly condenses on the seeds. This is not a problem if the whole of the seed sample is to be sown, but it is if the container is left open for the bulk of the seed sample to get a hoar frost coating. Water is then sealed in and re-frozen and this is far from ideal. Hence, if only a few seeds are required, try to remove them from the seed container while still in the frozen atmosphere of the refrigerator rather than at room temperature.

Modification of the storage atmosphere surrounding the seed to reduce the O_2 would also reduce levels of respiration. This is only effective if the seed is dry; otherwise anaerobic reactions may occur. The longevity of a seed sample in storage is influenced by the temperature at which seeds are stored and their moisture content during this period.

Storage of plant material is often affected by reductions in the level of atmospheric oxygen but in seed storage this factor is of minor significance when compared with temperature and moisture levels, although increases in carbon dioxide concentrations may have more influence.

For successful storage the seed must be 'mature', that is with a developed embryo and a stable food reserve. It may also be relevant to indicate that fungi will be active at a moisture content of more than 12% to 14% - even at relatively low levels of temperature - and precautions such as seed dressings may be necessary to prevent losses from fungal infections under these circumstances.

Seed: The Effects of Ageing and Loss in Viability

- Degradation of cellular membranes and subsequent loss of control of permeability. (The seed coats may soften excessively and flood the embryo with water.)

- Impairment of energy-yielding mechanisms – the enzymes may have lost quality.

- Reduced respiration and biosynthesis – the enzymes may have lost quality.

- Slower germination and seedling growth. [One year I grew onions from second year seed, stored in my garden shed. The onions germinated but the result was much poorer than the crop from some fresh onion seed sown at the same time – ONM.].

- Reduced storage potential.

- Slower growth and development of the plant.

- Less uniformity of growth and development in the population.

- Increased susceptibility to environmental stresses and diseases.

- Increase in percentage of abnormal seedlings.

- Loss in germination ability.

Seed Banks

The use of seed banks – such as the one at The Royal Botanic Gardens, Kew – aim to conserve the world's flora for generations to use in centuries to come. Research at Reading University, using accelerated ageing techniques and the application of a seed viability model, has identified cereals as among the longest-lived seeds and certain tree species as the shortest lived. It has predicted that if seeds of barley and mahogany are stored at $-18^{\circ}C$ and 5% moisture content, the time for the viability to decline from 90% to 50% is 1300 years and 53 years respectively.

4. PROPAGATION BY SEED

The **advantages** or reasons why growing plants from seed is well worthwhile include:

1. It is a low cost, mass production system.
2. The relatively low levels of pests and diseases which may come in the "packet" with the seeds.
3. New types of plants may be produced.
4. F_1 hybrids provide a source of "true to type" plants frequently with hybrid vigour and a natural abundance of health and earliness.
5. Seeds usually provide a cheap and easy way of storing and transporting a plant.

The **disadvantages** of seeds may include:

1) There may be uncertainties over germination and seed raising.
2) Due to the unreliability of some varieties which may be grown, it is difficult to guarantee a true to type plant.
3) Plant production may be slow.
4) Some double flowers produce very little viable seed.

The syllabus content is reasonably clear and it may be that the groups of seeds may generally be considered as:

Large:	includes beans, peas, maize
Medium:	parsnip, carrot, brassica
	may include Zinnia, Dahlia and Borage
Fine:	the bent grasses, Begonia, Petunia and conceivably fern spores (which strictly speaking are not seeds at all)

SEED SOWING OUTDOORS

Vast numbers of plants are raised by sowing seeds in drills out-of-doors. It is a low cost technique, very useful indeed where the value of the seed is not so high that the loss of a few seedlings will be catastrophic.

The advantage of sowing in containers is largely one of greater control; out-of-doors there is little one can do about the weather and larger pests may be problematic like field slugs, let alone the depredations of birds, deer or sheep.

Some seeds have an agricultural level of vigour and these may be drilled in the open using a range of seed drill types – the Planet Junior is illustrated below, also a Brush drill.

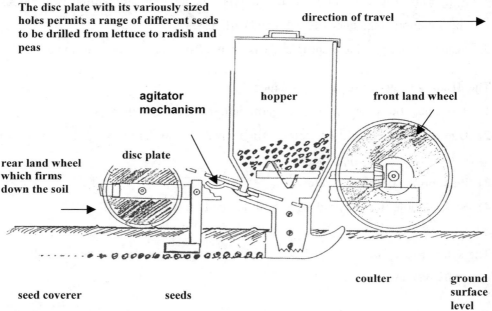

The disc plate with its variously sized holes permits a range of different seeds to be drilled from lettuce to radish and peas

direction of travel

agitator mechanism

hopper

front land wheel

disc plate

rear land wheel which firms down the soil

coulter

ground surface level

seed coverer

seeds

Figure 10 : A random seeder (typical design) Planet Junior

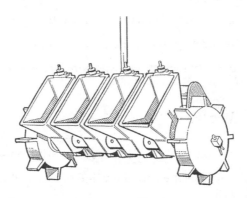

Figure 11: Small hand held seed drill - used for sowing in trays in cold frames

The seedbed has to be well prepared - that is it should be cultivated to produce a firm, fine tilth with a soil moisture content close to field capacity; a level of fertility with index levels for nutrients close to 0 (i.e. no further nutrients required), and with a pH suitable for the crop, e.g. 6.5 to 7.0 for most garden vegetables.

The setting of the seed drill requires care and should take into account the nature of the seedbed. If it is more cloddy in structure as a result of difficult weather conditions when preparing the seedbed, it might be set to drill the seeds a little deeper. Also moisture levels are a little higher at the deeper levels so the larger medium-sized seeds like beetroot might be sown at 28 to 30mm deep, while lettuce might still do well at 15mm deep.

The rate of sowing would take into account an assessment of the seedbed condition – its warmth, moisture and the quality of the tilth. Drilling at a marginally heavier rate can partially compensate for poorer sowing conditions.

The space between the rows may depend on a range of many factors, such as the crop's final size, e.g. carrots need less space than cabbages. In the row a carrot to be grown for bunching might need 40mm x 20mm and a large carrot 40mm x 40mm. Whereas to grow to final cropping, i.e. direct drilled cabbage to produce a cabbage weighing about 0.8kg, a space of 500mm x 500mm would be helpful.

The weed control programme has to be considered. Mechanical hoeing systems may require 300mm between the rows as a minimum. Sometimes harvesting is a factor, e.g. runner beans when grown up supports – the hard-working harvester needs space and up to 1 metre between twin rows is not unreasonable.

In general wider spacing is helpful in the production of larger heavier crop sizes – big vegetables. It also helps when there are dry growing conditions because there is relatively more soil available for exploitation by the roots searching for water.

The market requirements are fickle and when crops are grown it may be that the sales outlets require miniature vegetables – extra tender and fresh – or they may need huge onions or whatever to make the large onion rings!

Sowing Seeds Out of Doors – A Discussion:

Broad Bean (as an example of a large seed)

- Soil preparation - select land that has been manured and well dug over in the autumn/early winter. The pH should be close to 6.5. Break down the soil to a fine tilth just before sowing. A base dressing of N:P:K may be required.

- Prepare seed drills - 450mm apart and 75mm deep. Sow the seeds at c.225mm spacings or, if in double rows, space the rows at 300mm and leave 600mm between the twin rows. Cover the seed and firm.

- Cultivation of the young crop - hoe for weed control as may be necessary. Blackfly may invade the crop – some control may be obtained by pinching out infested tops. Sprays with soft soap or other pesticide may be required. The pea and bean weevil is usually present as a minor pest causing minor notches on foliage. In severe circumstances pesticide attention might be required or some sort of sticky trap devised. Broad beans respond well to some herbicidal programmes.

[Examination candidates should be aware that although the syllabus is devised so that each paragraph is specific in its assessment criteria, there is every likelihood that the questions may link several areas together. So, in the case of the Broad bean, the question might actually approach the crop management of this bean from rotation and crop planning; soil preparation and sowing; various cultivations like hoeing. It may also include site, varieties, nutrition, pests and diseases, harvesting and post crop - removal of the haulm and how to look after the land thereafter.]

Beetroot (as an example of a smaller seed)

In this crop the seeds are sown to grow to harvest "in situ". This is typical of root crops (carrots, parsnips) and onions raised from seed (as against sets). For some other smaller seeds, like cabbages, cauliflowers, Brussels sprouts and early lettuce, it is more usual to raise the seedlings in a seedbed and transplant them to their cropping positions.

- Soil preparation – beetroot (and carrots) would normally follow crops which had had bulky organic manures. The soil would have had an autumn digging or ploughing and a spring tilling to prepare a firm, fine, well prepared seedbed. Some base fertilisers may be desirable depending on the soil's requirements for NPK. Typically, a National Growmore type of compound could be applied at $100g/m^2$ and this would be spread evenly and worked in with the final cultivations in the seedbed preparation.

- Sowing date – April and May to early June. Space rows 300mm apart. Sow thinly and leave the crop at around 100mm spacings after thinning, or closer if "baby beet" are required.

Nursery Seedbeds

For crops like cabbages that are to be transplanted, it is usual to have an area of nursery seedbed. The seedbed should be well cultivated and brought to a fine tilth. Extra care should be taken to ensure that the soil is in "good heart" – that it is in a fine well structured tilth with good levels of organic matter, well supplied in earlier years with FYM (farmyard manure). This would also provide good levels of the nutrients N, P and K, plus all the minor nutrients. The pH levels indicating good levels of available lime, e.g. pH 6.5 – 7.0.

The seedbed should be well firmed and raked over so that it presents a uniform opportunity for each seed when sown to germinate and grow well. Individual seed drills are prepared using a line and triangular or half moon draw hoe (or seed drill) at a spacing to suit the crop and seedbed management system. This might require the seed drills to be 150mm to 300mm or more apart. Seeds should be sown thinly, e.g. at 25mm spacings, in neat shallow drills of c.40mm - 50mm depth. The seed should be covered with earth and the area raked over.

In dry weather it may be necessary to water well. (Irrigate the seedbed site a day or two beforehand.) It is generally less helpful to irrigate after sowing because of the loss of soil structure and the stimulus from the water to encourage the weed seeds to grow.

The young plants would be lifted and transplanted to their cropping positions before they become drawn or hard (dry, brittle and starved due to the severe competition for light, space, water and nutrients.)

Outdoor seedbeds for a range of floral crops like wallflowers, sweet williams and *Myosotis* can be very valuable. Also the more specialised crops such as *Cyclamen hederifolium* and the woody plants including *Cotoneaster* and *Berberis* species and rose root stocks – *R. canina* – usually after a seed treatment to break the dormancy.

Very Fine Seeds

These seeds are usually sown in protected propagation areas because of the high cost of the seed and the difficulty in managing a crop of very small seedlings. Such seeds as *Nicotiana*, *Petunia*, *Begonia* and indeed pansy. The high value of each F_1 hybrid seed does merit the additional care and protection.

SOWING AFTER-CARE IN THE OPEN

The problems that may occur to seedbeds are legion but the usual difficulties include:

- Drought – it is always tricky to have to irrigate. Mist-like water distribution does little soil surface damage but larger droplets may lead to soil capping and poor germination.

- Pests – flea beetles and allied small leaf-eating pests – *Collembola* (the springtails), slugs, snails, rabbits and birds can be a big problem.

- Diseases – there tend to be few for seedlings in the field – very different under glass on occasion. Lettuce and marrows may suffer from mosaic virus. Brassicas from wire stem (*Corticium solani*). Blindness in cauliflowers due to a sudden chill (but this is a physiological disorder not a fungal problem).

- <u>Weeds</u> - field soils usually contain a huge number of weed seeds whose dormancy may be broken by the various tillages undertaken when preparing the seedbed which bring them up to the light.

- <u>Frost</u> - frost-tender species – runner beans, dwarf beans, tomatoes, cucumbers and marrows – will all require protection against frost once they "are up". Often this may only need to be minimal, even a newspaper may be enough protection but glass cloches are very good.

- <u>Wind</u> - severe winds cause desiccation and check growth.

CARE OF ESTABLISHED SEEDLINGS

The key issues are the availability of space, water, light and nutrients and freedom from competition from pests and diseases. Hence, avoid sowing excessively thickly and thin down the rows to give the plants ample **space**. This should also provide sufficient **light**. **Water** – endeavour to keep the root run up to field capacity. **Nutrients** - this is only likely to be a difficulty on poorly prepared seedbeds or where the substrate is a sand, grit, vermiculite or peat media lacking adequate nutritional supplements.

Pests and diseases – the control of the problems have to start with the identification of the difficulty that may then be addressed with a treatment programme. This may be a barrier like fleece, pesticides, predators, or other environmental improvements which assist in encouraging crop growth - e.g. by lowering the relative humidity which could be favouring a downy mildew. Competition from **weeds** may be serious and cultural, physical, mechanical or hand cultivation systems or chemical weed control may be considered.

COMPOSTS FOR SEEDS AND SUBSEQUENT GROWTH

Loam Composts

There are advantages and disadvantages to using loam-based composts and the decision as to whether or not to use them for a particular role may be quite difficult.

Loam is very good indeed for long-term operations, i.e. when seeds or plants may be in the same pot for more than 12 months.

In the late 1930s, the John Innes Horticultural Institute produced a standard series of recipes for composts that were loam-based. The materials used were closely specified in order to produce uniform results

- Loam:

  This should be medium to heavy turf loam which should be stacked with strawy manure for 6 months. Any lime deficiencies should be corrected by adding the appropriate quantity of ground limestone. The loam should then be sterilised, preferably by steam. The pH should be 6.3 (slightly acid) and the loam should be screened through a 9mm sieve.

- Peat:

  This should be moist, granulated moss peat with a pH of 4.0 – 4.5 and sifted as above.

- Sand (grit):

  This should be washed, free from lime or chalk, sharp and coarse. 60 – 70% of the particles should be between 1.5mm and 3mm in size. There are four John Innes Compost recipes - a seed compost and three potting composts.

John Innes Seed Compost (JIS)

2 parts loam
1 part peat   } by volume
1 part sand (grit)

1.10kg superphosphate
550g chalk or ground limestone   } per m^3 of mix

JIS(A) has sulphur in lieu of the $CaCO_3$ and is useful for plants which require acid soil conditions.

John Innes Potting Compost (JIP)

There are three different grades, each containing a different fertiliser (see below).

Each consists of: 7 parts loam
                         3 parts peat
                         2 parts sand (grit)

Plus:

JIP 1   2.75kg base fertiliser*
        550g chalk per m^3 of mix

JIP 2   5.50kg base fertiliser*
        1.10kg chalk per m^3 of mix

JIP 3   8.25kg base fertiliser*
        1.65kg chalk per m^3 of mix

* The base fertiliser is a mix by weight of:
        **Hoof and Horn (13% N) 2 parts
        Superphosphate (18% P_2O_5) 2 parts
        Sulphate of potash (48% K_2O) 1 part.

** NB. With the demise of the use of bovine sourced organic fertilisers due to BSE and human health, the Hoof and Horn could be substituted with 2 parts fish meal.

One ration of fertiliser and lime made up the mix for John Innes Potting Compost No. 1, two rations for John Innes Potting Compost No. 2, also a No. 3. The extra fertilisers provided much more plant nutrient and would keep a plant growing well for longer.

Loamless Compost

These have become more widely used as loam has become scarce and for economic reasons. Loamless composts may be "peat and sand" based, 100% peat based or may include other materials.

The Glasshouse Crops Research Institute formulated the following composts:

Constituents	Seed compost	GCRI potting composts			
	A	B General Use	C Winter (c)	D Summer	E High P (b) longer term use
% by volume					
Peat : Sand ratio	50 : 50	75 : 25	75 : 25	75 : 25	75 : 25
Base dressing kg/m^3					
Ammonium nitrate	0	0.4	-	-	0.2
Urea formaldehyde (a)	-	-	0.5	1.0	-
Magnesium ammonium phosphate	-	-	-	-	1.5
Potassium nitrate	0.4	0.75	0.75	0.75	0.4
Normal superphosphate	0.75	1.5	1.5	1.5	-
Ground chalk or limestone	3.0	2.25	2.25	2.25	2.25
Ground magnesium limestone	-	2.25	2.25	2.25	2.25
Fritted trace elements WM 55	-	0.4	0.4	0.4	0.4
Approximate nutrient content g/m^3 (=mg/litre)					
Soluble N	56	241	105	105	124
Insoluble N	Nil	Nil	190	380	75
Phosphorus (P)	59	119	119	119	152
Potassium (K)	146	274	274	274	132

[I don't think that this has to be learned, but knowledge of the GCRI mixes is a foundation stone in considering soilless media for protected cropping – ONM.]

Table 4 : GCRI compost formulations

(a) Composts containing urea formaldehyde should not be stored longer than 7 days.

(b) For longer term crops where there is a risk of phosphorus deficiency and liquid feeding with phosphate is not desired, it may be helpful to use a commercial magnesium ammonium phosphate fertiliser. This also contains 11% K_2O.

(c) To provide quicker drainage in winter for pot chrysanthemums, the proportion of sand (grit) may be increased to 33%.

Other Materials used in Loamless Composts:

1. **Bark** – pulverised bark has been introduced in the UK as compost material. It has been widely used since the 1960's in Canada, USA and Scandinavia. It is important that the bark is stored for a few weeks to remove any risk of infection from rhizomorphs of *Armillaria mellea*. Conifer bark may contain toxic turpines which takes eight weeks of composting at 90°C to reduce levels to acceptable amounts. Bark does have a slow rate of breakdown and retains moisture, though it is difficult to re-wet once allowed to dry out. The pH of bark varies from 4.1 with "Cambark" to 6.8 with "Forest Bark".

2. **Rockwool** – blocks of rockwool are used for cuttings and growing on, the blocks being transplanted into larger blocks when the roots are sufficiently developed. Rockwool is made from 60% Diabas (granite), 20% limestone, 20% coke, melted at 1,600°C to produce fibres which are then joined using a binding and wetting agent. Granulated rockwool is now being produced which can be mixed with peat or used on its own. It does not break down easily.

3. **Perlite** - is an alumino-silicate of volcanic origin. When it is crushed and heated rapidly to 1000°C it expands to form white, lightweight aggregates which are stable and do not break down in composts. It is chemically inert, sterile, has a neutral pH and high water-holding capacity (it can hold 3 to 4 times its own weight in water). It requires less watering than sand or grit but excess water can drain away to provide good aeration.

It is now widely used as a cutting and seed mix used with peat; as a growing medium for potting, and as a soil conditioner, especially in Japan and the USA. Its thermal properties give good insulation for the storage of dahlia tubers for example. It is also used in hydroponics and Nutrient Film Technique (NFT). Perlite is available in several grades – supercoarse, superfine, standard and seed grade.

4.   **Vermiculite** – this is an aluminium, iron, magnesium silicate which, when put through a high temperature furnace, produces flakes of material each containing thousands of tiny air cells. It is sterile, light and improves drainage and aeration. The plate-like scales can break down in two years, or less if mixed with sand or grit. It is used in seed composts, for rooting cuttings, in micro-propagation and twin scaling of bulbs.

Figure 12: Vermiculite

Vermiculite looks like soil crumbs but is made up of flakes which open up like a concertina to hold a quantity of water available to plant roots.

<u>Peat Free:</u>

The organic lobby have largely succeeded in making Peat an unattractive soil media. Hence the great demand for Peat Free compost. In time there will be a reliable range of mixes which use no peat. The capacity of the organic materials like peat to have colloidal properties as well as – in the case of moss peat – a huge air filled porosity does make peat hard to replace in bulk sources, rather than smaller scale compost as in town refuse composts – which may have an element of variability in their performance.

Methods of Seed Sowing – some useful Techniques

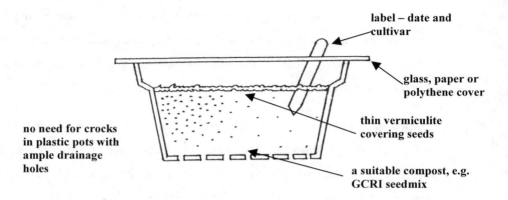

label – date and cultivar

glass, paper or polythene cover

thin vermiculite covering seeds

no need for crocks in plastic pots with ample drainage holes

a suitable compost, e.g. GCRI seedmix

Figure 13: Seeds sown in a shallow pan (150mm) and covered with a sheet of glass

c. 50mm

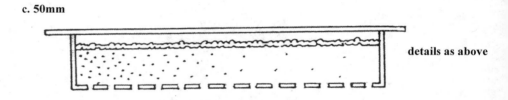

details as above

Figure 14: Seed sowing in a plastic seed tray

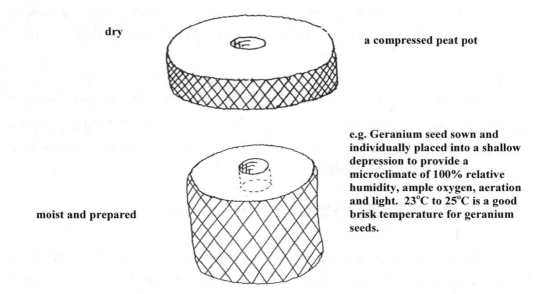

dry

a compressed peat pot

moist and prepared

e.g. Geranium seed sown and individually placed into a shallow depression to provide a microclimate of 100% relative humidity, ample oxygen, aeration and light. 23°C to 25°C is a good brisk temperature for geranium seeds.

Figure 15: Seed sown in a jiffy pot

The compost has to provide a suitable resting place. The ideal depth of sowing is important because at this position the seed is held adequately so that the thrust of the radicle is contained without dislodging the seed. Also the energy of the germinating seed is not dissipated in the etiolation of the epicotyl (or hypocotyl in some seeds) as it grows through too great a depth of "earth" cover.

SOWING SEEDS IN CONTAINERS

N.B: For some pot plants and bedding plant seeds, germination temperatures matter greatly, e.g. *Geranium, Begonia, Gloxinia.* Temperature measurements should be taken where the seeds actually are placed, i.e. the bulb of the thermometer precisely in amongst the seed in the media in the container.

All the seeds require a suitable media for growth and development. The loamless mixes tend to have better air, AFP (air filled porosity) and water holding capacity, even 50%+ for some materials like Rockwool.

There is still a case for loam-based mixes and the most famous of these are the John Innes series. Seeds may be sown both in the Seed mix and in the Potting mix (JIP1) for robust seeds.

When the seeds have been sown it is necessary to wait for the germination. This can be very speedy - just a few days, or up to three weeks or so for parsnips. (Earlier emergence is possible if seeds have been chitted and fluid-drilled as has been mentioned earlier in Section 2.)

AFTER CARE OF SEEDS SOWN IN CONTAINERS

When the container is located in a protected environment located under cover – as in a glasshouse or polytunnel – the seedlings have to be given close attention. They require water, light, warmth and nutrients, CO_2 and relative freedom from competition from other crop members, pests, diseases and weeds.

Water can be supplied via a capillary watering system, or via a hose and rose, or via more sophisticated systems including "travelling" gantry systems.

Light and enough shade to reduce stress can come via the glasshouse canopy but in the winter period the light levels are low and the day length short. Timed periods of supplementary lighting can, for high value crops, be used to provide the extra light needed for photosynthesis. Cheaper to provide in energy terms, is night-break lighting which tends to encourage sensitive plants to react as if they were growing in a period of short nights/long days.

Nutrients can be supplied via the irrigation unit or by controlled-release fertilisers (CRF) already mixed into the media.

CO_2 There are considerable benefits for some economic crops which may result from the use of supplementary CO_2 during daylight hours and when the temperatures are high, e.g. over c.22°C because the crops are able to gain considerably in their dry weight and this really shows in larger stronger plants.

SEED SOWING – HARDY PLANTS

Most Mediterranean species germinate in the autumn after the first rain. This works well with their mild winters but for the UK climate sowing hardy species in the early part of the new year and standing them outside to take the chill of winter has much to commend it. Glass frame lights with their increased warmth could go on in early April.

A useful system is to use 90mm plastic half pots of good quality. Not every seed pan will germinate in the first spring. This system with the pea grit on top will provide the conditions for stratification of the seeds over the following winter(s). A cool North border frame situation is useful.

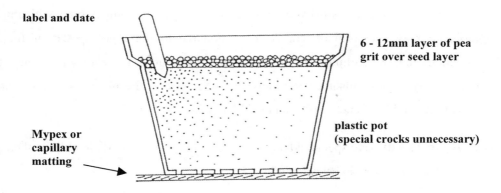

Figure 16: Sowing the seeds of slow germinating hardy plants in pots

Heat sterilisation of the soil will reduce the weed and pest competitors.

This system provides the essential conditions for germination – viable seed, adequate warmth (for hardy plants), moisture, oxygen, light for light-requiring species and, perversely enough, dark for those with a dark requirement. Plus light for the seedlings after emergence, a suitable resting place, relative freedom from pests, diseases and weeds plus a relatively low competition for water from the soluble salt concentration in the compost.

Once the seedlings are established they could be nursed in "waiting beds" spaced at 50mm or 75mm square, or in frames of good soil. Always try and grow a few spare to 'swop', but to try and grow all that may come up could be a self-inflicted disaster.

Once up, the seedlings can benefit from higher fertility with composts like John Innes Potting Compost No.1, supplemented with slow-release fertilisers such as Osmocote 3 to 6 months (or Ficote or Vitax Q4 or ENMag). Faster growth rates can be achieved in the mixes of forest bark with peat and slow-release fertilisers now popular for container grown plants.

SEED SOWING – TENDER SPECIES

The same rules apply as to hardy plants but attention to the germination temperature most suited to the species is likely to be rewarded. Warmer temperatures with ample moisture may also provide conditions conducive to the rapid spread of fungal infections like the damping-off group of fungi. Attention to detail will reduce the opportunity for establishment of these competitors and the use of a suitable pre-sowing fungicidal drench can be a considerable help.

F_1 **Hybrid seeds** have special advantages which may outweigh their additional cost. The advantages of F_1 hybrids include:

- True to type
- Hybrid vigour
- Earliness

It is the true to type quality that is so attractive, enabling uniformity in, for example, a bed of tender geraniums, to be as good as if they had been raised traditionally (from cuttings).

F_1 hybrids are the first cross of two true breeding parent lines.

In the classical experiments carried out by Gregor Mendel (published in 1865 and 1866) he crossed true breeding, tall growing peas (shown TT below) with dwarf growing peas (shown tt). The tall character is dominant over the recessive character of dwarfness.

Most parent plants are diploids – that is they have two sets of chromosomes*, so that when the ovules or pollen grains are produced each ovule or pollen grain has just one set.

Parents TT		tt	The pollen and the ovules only have half the genetic complement, i.e. T or t.
Parental gametes	T ↓x t		All the peas are tall (the T being dominant over the dwarf)
F_1 generation (the first cross)	T t		

In this F_1 generation all the progeny were tall growing peas.

* Effectively each chromosome represents a characteristic such as tallness or shortness. Usually there is a dominant characteristic such as tallness over shortness.

DISEASES AND DAMPING-OFF

Seeds may suffer from diseases from the time of sowing until establishment. There are soil-borne, air-borne and seed-borne diseases. The general principles of good husbandry include the following:

- **Hygiene** - Maintain very high standards. Sterilised compost, clean benches and standing areas. Use new or sterilised trays or pots, keep seed trays off the ground. Prick out healthy seedlings from trays/pans and discard the others. Avoid overcrowding and overwatering.

Use mains water, from a hose and rose rather than a dip can and rose because of the risk of debris from rainwater tanks. (There is nothing wrong with rainwater but there can be problems during and after its collection.) Use sterilised or new capillary matting.

- When using fungicides, identify the problem so far as this is possible so that the most suitable fungicide approved for its use can be used.

- Provide as ideal/optimum conditions for germination as can be arranged.

The diseases include:

- Soil-borne - *Pythium* and *Phytophthora*

Irrigation water is the most important carrier of secondary infections. Also around, causing damping-off, are *Rhizoctonia*, **Blackroot rot,** *Fusarium* **and** *Sclerotinia*.

Air-borne - *Botrytis* and **Powdery Mildew**

Contamination usually comes from older infected plant material close by.

Seed-borne - *Alternaria* and *Septoria*

Seed-borne diseases are rarely a problem from seeds supplied in the normal way. Copper fungicides help with *Pythium* and *Phytophthora*. Fewer control pesticides (chemicals) are available to amateurs than to commercial growers.

For the latest lists refer to the current edition of the UK Pesticide Guide, published by The British Crop Protection Council, BCPC Publications Sales, Bear Farm, Binfield, Bracknell, Berkshire, UK, RG12 5QE (Phone or Fax 0118-934-2727).

Non-professional users really have to defend their seedlings with the more limited range of pesticides available from garden centres, shops and other postal sources. If the quality of the hygiene system in operation is excellent then the only major source of contamination from fungi will be from the seeds themselves and fortunately this does not represent a great threat in the normal way.

5.   RELEVANCE OF PLANT ANATOMY AND PHYSIOLOGY TO VEGETATIVE PROPAGATION

The basic botany is set out in our Lesson 4 (Reference to H.C.C. Advanced Certificate in Horticulture Course programme) – Plant Taxonomy, Morphology and Anatomy, also the Plant Physiology in Lesson 6. In a very real sense the cultivation and propagation of plants is applied science. An outline understanding of what the various parts of the plants require does aid the propagator to get closer to the optimum resources and reduce the problems of over and under provision.

THE ROLE OF CAMBIUM

These are the cells that can heal plant wounds by producing callus tissue. From these and from the stems near to the cuts adventitious roots may arise. The activities of the cambium are stimulated by hormones produced by the meristems – the regions at the tips of the shoots (the growing points) and buds in the leaf axils. Supplementary hormones are often used by propagators to stimulate callus tissue. Wounding the basal area exposes more cambium tissue and this can aid root establishment hugely for some species, e.g. *Hydrangea paniculata*.

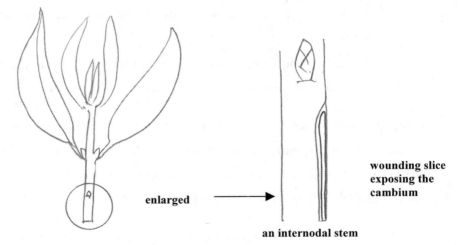

enlarged

an internodal stem

wounding slice exposing the cambium

Figure 17: Cutting of *Hydrangea paniculata*

When grafting it is the cambium tissue that is critical to the successful union. The cambium cells from the stock and the scion of compatible species are able to work together to produce new tissues of phloem and xylem.

The latter provides the woody link (for woody species) and the long xylem cells give a mechanical strength that increases over the first year or two to give a sturdy union. As well as providing the water and nutrients for the transpiration stream.

From the new cells come the whole set of tissues that heal the wounds and grow together neatly but the cells do not mix significantly, hence the wood above and below the union exhibits the characteristics each had prior to the grafting operation. (There is more about grafting in Section 8.)

THE STEM, NODE AND INTERNODE

The stem carries the plant's buds and leaves – mainly above ground but in some instances below ground, such as the rhizomes of iris or couch grass. Leaves grow from **nodes** spaced along the stem and the **axil** is the point at which they join. The spaces on a stem between the nodes are called internodes. A true leaf on a stem has a bud in its axil (an **axillary bud**). This is horticulturally significant because:

- Stems are usually solid at the node.
- There are more natural hormones present which are able to assist with wound healing.
- The axillary bud itself has its own **meristem** and this is able to generate new hormones that may assist with growth and development of the tissues.

Most propagators would choose to make the cut just below the node because the success of this technique is well proven. Making a wounding cut as mentioned earlier under cambium can be very rewarding but it does also increase the risk of fungal and other diseases entering the larger area of the cut.

Roots do not only arise from the basal cut but from the whole of the base of the stem area. It seems that **root primordia** may exist in the stems and these may in part be mechanically restricted by the tough outer bark tissues. Some propagators make slit cuts as their method of wounding and certainly roots may simply burst through these slits in a most satisfactory way.

BULBS

Bulblets

A scooped Hyacinth. The bulb consists of a short stem, modified leaves and the growing point. By removing the basal plate completely (that is the stem in reality), the bulb is able to generate bulblets from the cut leaf bases.

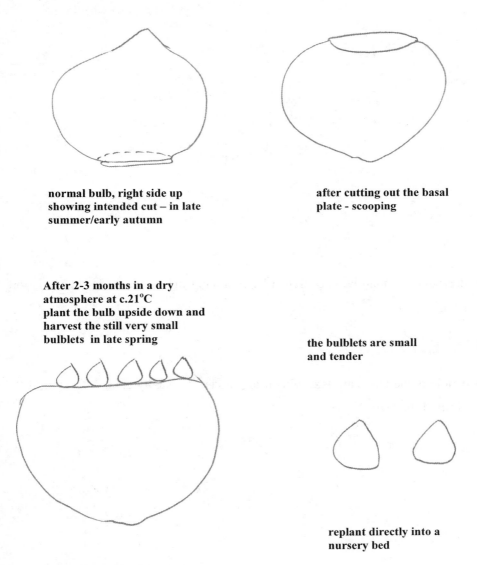

normal bulb, right side up
showing intended cut – in late
summer/early autumn

after cutting out the basal
plate - scooping

After 2-3 months in a dry
atmosphere at c.21°C
plant the bulb upside down and
harvest the still very small
bulblets in late spring

the bulblets are small
and tender

replant directly into a
nursery bed

Figure 18: A scooped Hyacinth

(Please also see illustration and notes in Section 8 on the twin scaling of *Narcissus*

Bulbils

These are small bulbs that may grow in the axils of the leaves of some lilies, e.g. *Lilium auratum, L. longiflorum, L.bulbiferum*. They may be harvested in the late summer and potted immediately into a suitable mix with loam, peat or its equivalent and grit, or a proprietary loamless mix, or JIP1.

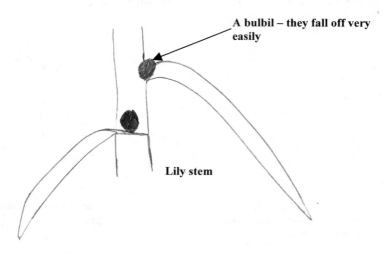

A bulbil – they fall off very easily

Lily stem

Bulbil production may be encouraged by removing the flower buds shortly before flowering.

THE PETIOLE

The petiole is the leaf stalk that joins it to a node. It usually is an extension of the central rib of the leaf.

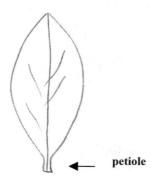

petiole

Quite a number of leaves can be induced to root at the petiole but relatively few species are able to grow to become a plant. However, members of the *Gesneriaceae* family, the African Violet, *Gloxinia*, *Gesnera* and *Streptocarpus*, also *Peperomia* (*Piperaceae*) may be propagated from leaf petioles and *Begonia rex* (*Begoniaceae*) but *B. rex* more usually is derived from foliar embryos.

Monocot Leaves

A number of monocotyledon leaves, *Hyacinth*, *Lachenalia*, *Leucojum*, *Galanthus*, *Endymion* and *Scilla* have an inherent capacity to produce a plantlet following a cut to a vein on a suitable leaf.

LEAF CUTTINGS

One system is to cut up a leaf into large postage stamp sized pieces. Lay these flat on the surface of a suitable propagating media, e.g. 50/50 peat and grit, in shade, under mist or in a closed propagating case at c.22°C. Plantlets arise at the cut veins and from the central "hub" of the veins where the petiole joins the lamina (leaf blade).

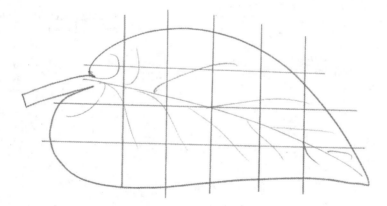

Figure 19: Mature leaf of *Begonia rex* – leaf blade cutting

There are other ways of cutting up the leaf - or indeed of leaving it whole - but this system does enable individual units of the plant to be potted up with whole leaves.

It can be so difficult to manage to divide up the leaf with lots of little plantlets all with their frail roots – or not – so that one is able to get a few good plants out of the whole assembly. Growing on will require warm conditions (20 – 25°C) with good light but sunless conditions, plenty of space and high humidity. Compost for pot plants and liquid feeds.

N.B. There is no advantage in using leaf cuttings to propagate the variegated plant forms because the tissues that generate the new plant do not come from the epidermis where the attractive coloured leaf form is located but from the regenerated cambium cells in the inner part of the leaf.

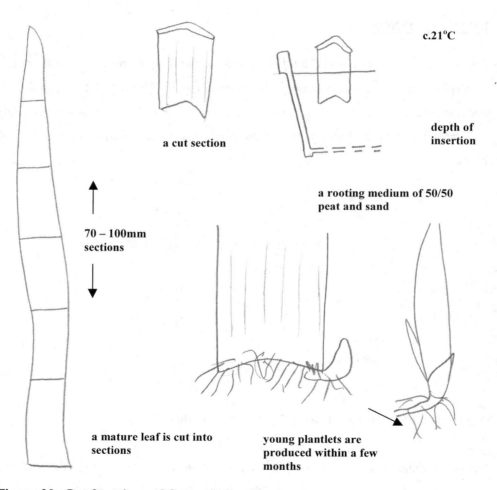

c.21°C

a cut section

depth of insertion

a rooting medium of 50/50 peat and sand

70 – 100mm sections

a mature leaf is cut into sections

young plantlets are produced within a few months

Figure 20: Leaf cuttings of *Sansevieria trifasciata*

Foliar Embryos

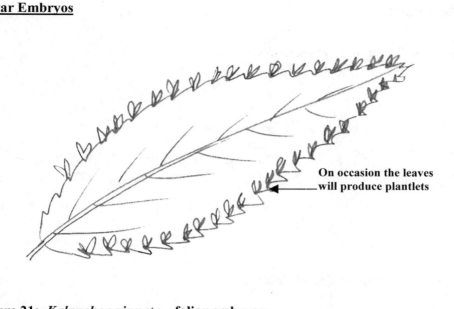

On occasion the leaves will produce plantlets

Figure 21: *Kalanchoe pinnata* – **foliar embryos**

Foliar embryos are useful for the production of:

- *Tolmiea menziesii*
- *Sedum spectabile*
- *Kalanchoe pinnata*
- *Begonia rex*

- *Asplenium bulbiferum* (fern) ⎫
- *Polystichum setiferum* ⎬ both produce bulbils
  ⎭

For your own researches, please see if you can resource some of these plants and propagate a few. It is fun. The capacity to draw them from life may also be useful practice.

Root Cuttings

These can be useful for *Primula denticulata*

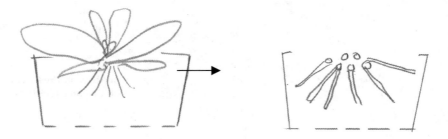

Figure 22a: Root cutting of *Primula*

Leaving the plant in situ and removing all the top to expose only the roots may seem very drastic but the tops of the roots can regenerate plants. So, in place of the one plant there may be a dozen or so. (The removed top may also be ready to re-root.)

More usually the roots of *Anchusa* are used, also *Limonium* and for choice *Verbascum* cultivars. (Do look up some cultivars in catalogues or in the RHS Plant Finder.) Some shrubs grow well from roots - especially *Rhus typhina* which is unstoppable if spreading under the fence from your neighbour. It is very useful for student practicals because there are usually plenty of root pieces available and everyone's "pot" will grow!

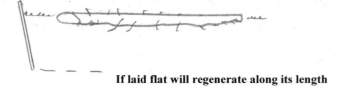

If laid flat will regenerate along its length

Figure 22b: Root cutting of *Rhus typhina*

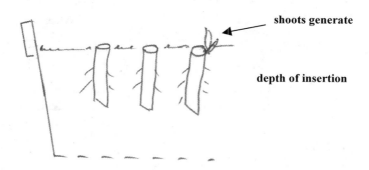

shoots generate

depth of insertion

Figure 23: Angle of root cutting

It is traditional to have an angled cut at the bottom and a flat cut at the top. This is helpful because the root will have its polarity and even if placed upside down, the cut naturally uppermost will endeavour to produce the shoots.

The properties that make a root suitable for propagation include:

i)   The natural propensity for the root to be able to generate adventitious roots. (We are all familiar with this capacity in the hoed off dandelion and daisy. However not all weeds or plants are able to recover from such hoeing off of the top growth.)

ii)   The nutritional status of the plant. In general high carbohydrate levels are associated with good regeneration vigour.

iii)   The polarity of the cutting – with the natural flow of auxins to the base of the cutting. Gibberellic acid and cytokinins synthesised in the roots move upwards and are available to support shoots and leaves.

iv)   Light is a factor and some dim light is desirable for the top of the root cutting.

v)   The size of the propagule itself.

Roots are generated from the region of endodermal cylinder – this can often be seen if an old carrot is cut lengthways.

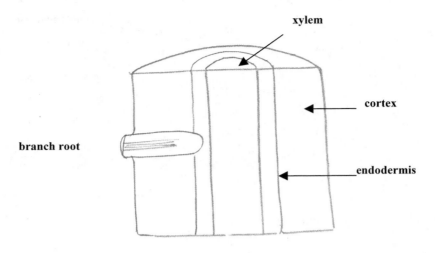

Figure 24: Section of cut carrot showing internal tissues

THE AXILLARY BUD

Possibly the best known example of this is the bud or chip bud used in producing roses, fruit trees and many woody ornamental trees, including *Prunus* cultivars, by budding – a form of grafting. (Please see Section 8)

There is an axillary bud at the base of every leaf. It has the potential to grow into a shoot. That not every bud does so is the result of the hormones that ensure the apical dominance of the shoot tip. If the stem tip is cut off the high concentration of auxins moving down the stem is removed and the inhibition to the growth of the axillary buds is removed.

This is what happens in effect when pruning apples in December or rose bushes in late March. By cutting back the stems to a bud this bud is much more likely to grow out. A similar effect can be seen in apple trees where, if a young shoot that was previously upright is tied down to a horizontal position, the axillary buds may develop into blossom buds and later these may develop shoots.

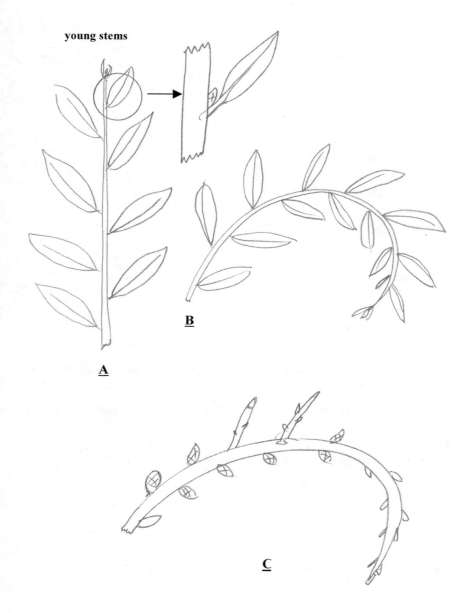

young stems

A

B

C

Figure 25: Axillary buds

A   The shoot growing vertically will tend to grow upwards with the lateral suppressed.

B   Where the shoot is horizontal or tied down, the axillary buds develop – differently. In the case of apples the axillary buds may develop into fruit buds, i.e. packed with 5 blossom buds and a rosette of leaves waiting to grow out in the spring.

C   Illustrating the same branch as B but at the end of the season. Some of the buds are now the fat fruit buds and others have developed into shoots. This is because the gravitational flow downwards of hormones from the growing tip has not happened and the suppression of the development of the axillary buds has not occurred. In a similar way pruning off a growing tip does alter the way the plant hormones may influence growth and development.

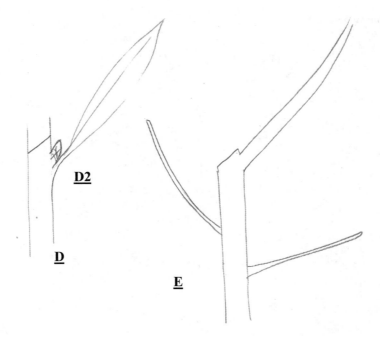

D2

D

E

D   If the shoot is pruned off just above the bud at D2, the flow of hormones is cut off and the bud is able to grow out.

E   The possible growth from the top three axillary buds as seen at the end of the growing season.

(For a chip bud grafting diagram please see Section 8.)

Some plants will grow from axillary bud cuttings. Examples include:

- Vine (*Vitis*) 'eyes'
- *Hedera helix*
- *Ficus elastica*
- Roses

Stem split in half

Which of these 'eyes' will root when given the right conditions ?

Part of the difficulty in using these small propagules for plant production is, in the case of roses for example:

i)   The tender nature of the cutting material.

ii)   The large cut surface increasing the risk of pathogen problems.

iii) The time taken to achieve a saleable plant.

The advantages where the system can be made to work include:

i)   The speed by which the numbers of plants in the clone can be increased.

ii)   The abundance of the bud wood material.

iii) The low cost per unit of this intensive production system.

The Importance of the Physiological Process of Transpiration, Respiration and Photosynthesis to Vegetative Propagation

TRANSPIRATION

It is almost always the case that every effort should be made to prevent water loss from cuttings by transpiration. (The exceptions might include some geraniums very prone to rotting at the stem base where a period of drying does cause the cut to seal which may secure survival even if it technically delays rooting.)

Shortage of water within the plant tissue leads directly to stress and stressed plant cells tend not to thrive but to close down the stomata which cuts down on photosynthesis and this stops the production of readily available energy from the sugars which would have been synthesised by leafy cuttings. Dormant wood cuttings should also be treated with care but at least they have good carbohydrate food reserves.

A cut stem with leaves on is going to lose water to the surrounding atmosphere all too easily. The only way that this water can be replaced is through the cut base of the stem. Very few plants will root as cuttings in water and yes, we all know of *Oleander*, *Salix*, *Geranium* and African Violet leaves and no doubt more, like flowering current, but these are the exceptions. Cut stems in water behave badly over time – as can be seen from such material placed in a vase. The cells at the base of the stem die through loss of oxygen and the excess of water upsetting their osmotic pressure. Pathogens move in.

The steps that can be taken to ensure that the cuttings (and 'bud wood') are as turgid as possible include:

1. Watering the plant the day before.
2. Harvesting the cutting material at daybreak.
3. Putting the material directly into a wet polybag, out of the sun and ideally in a chilled container.
4. Removal of the surplus leaves.

These efforts are primarily to ensure that with an environment of 100% relative humidity an absolute minimum of water will be lost.

When preparing the cuttings the same pattern of care should follow a similar procedure. Dull, cool, humid conditions are much kinder to the plant tissues than hot, dry, airy (windy) rooms and passageways.

It is not that wilted cutting material won't revive – a lot will, as in pansy cuttings and no doubt many others. It is that every check to growth is just that – a check and, if this can be avoided, success is more likely.

RESPIRATION

This process continues all the time for living organisms. Mostly for cuttings we want the process to be as slow as possible until the roots have formed.

Faster respiration rates at the base of the cutting and at the region of the graft union can be achieved by raising the temperature at the base of the cutting to a previously established optimum temperature. This increase in respiration rate will encourage cell division for the healing of the wound, the production of callus tissue and the development of adventitious roots.

When cold storing cuttings, for use at a different season, e.g. building up the cuttings of chrysanthemums to enable a very large batch of plants to be grown to flower for a particular date, then it is possible to reduce respiration rates. This can be achieved by dark, cold conditions of high relative humidity and where some of the oxygen in the air has been replaced by CO_2 and a higher percentage of nitrogen.

In supermarkets many of the vegetables and fruits are sold in packs with a modified atmosphere and the system seems to work very well. It can also be interesting to endeavour to judge the age of cabbage or Brussels sprouts by the amount of callus tissue that they have generated between harvesting to the time of the point of sale.

[My guess is that some such vegetable commodities could be stored for many weeks - and I have handled a film wrapped green cabbage in apparently perfect condition stored for a year at an experimental station some years ago - ONM]

PHOTOSYNTHESIS

Most gardeners will, at some time, have taken too many leaves off a softwood stem cutting and seen what has happened - the fairly steady decline in the life of the cutting as it struggles to survive, usually unsuccessfully. (We all quite probably also have taken softwood stem cuttings which are too big and too leafy and also seen these decline. Could you say why for each circumstance? (See notes below.)

The importance of photosynthesis is that it provides the source of sugars within the plant which are the essential energy source for the development of new cells for wound healing, growth and development.

What may not be so obvious is that excessive light levels cause stress in the leaf. If the temperature of the leaf heats up beyond the temperature which the plant can tolerate, then the leaf area is scorched. Prior to that the stomata will have closed and there will have been a check to growth/rooting/development. Hence good propagators use shade – in polytents, tented mist and "open" bench mist. Milky film, the white polythene, is a useful step towards lowering this stress from excessive light levels. Also in addition, fleece is popular and the various sorts of mesh sold on the roll. These can be available in various densities (e.g. 50% shade, 80% shade).

-ooOoo-

Answers for the Question above

The leafless cutting is endeavouring to heal the cut surfaces, develop roots and create leaves to meet its emergency needs. The too big cutting is also trying to heal the cut surfaces and to supply all the leaves with moisture, all from its own resources and from what it can absorb through the cut surface in the compost. It can easily be too much and the cutting desiccates and dies.

Along with light for photosynthesis also comes the stimuli to grow and develop supplied by plant hormones developed at the shoot tips.

Parts of plants located in darkness are more likely to root.

Some very difficult to root species of shrubs have had their rooting response improved by putting the whole of the stock plant in darkness for a few days prior to the collection of the leafy cutting material. The period without light leads to an etiolation response that is very favourable to rooting.

6. CARE OF STOCK PLANTS

The objectives for the stock plant to have include:

1. Provision of sufficient propagation material at the right time of year.

2. That the clones used for the mother plants are:
   a) correctly named and of excellent provenance (the source of the plant)
   b) of the best form available, e.g. colour, habit, scent
   c) producing strong, healthy, vigorous, juvenile material for use
   d) free from pests (such as scale insects)

      free from fungal disease (such as apple canker)

      free from bacterial disease (such as bacterial canker)

      free from virus (such as mosaic virus).

Some of the objectives are achieved by growing the stock plants in a unit isolated from the rest of the nursery. An alternative (and somewhat riskier approach) is to collect the propagation material from the shoots of the current crop of rooting cuttings/grafts. This can be an excellent source but it may lead to a loss of control of the cultivar because if the plants do not flower while in the propagating unit, it may not be possible to check their identity. Even if great care is taken it could be quite possible to propagate a natural sport in this way – not true to type or properly described.

If the collection of the propagation material is made from mature plants growing in garden conditions, the success may be excellent but the challenges for rooting may be:

i)   loss of juvenility

ii)   variability in the size and shape of the material

iii) presence of pests and diseases

iv)   lateness of the production of material.

In the growing season, the earlier the cuttings can be rooted, the sooner they will be able to grow and establish. For example, a hardy ornamental woody plant rooted from a cutting taken in late April could be a shrub of some substance, 600mm – 800mm high and well furnished. Whereas if the cutting was collected from a mature plant, say in late July, the plant might be well rooted but, say, only 200mm high without any additional branching. Such lightweight plants may be difficult to over-winter.

Specialist producers may have some of their stock beds within frameworks of tunnel houses so that for the critical late winter/early spring to early summer months, the frameworks can be covered with polythene and as a result the growth shoots to be used for propagation are produced earlier. Maybe 4 to 6 weeks or more and this is in effect extra growing time in the late summer with much heavier, sturdier, taller plants produced. There can be further advantages of the cuttings produced under cover because there is more control of the water, nutrition, pests and diseases and day length.

JUVENILITY

The cycle of the life of the plant starts with the formation of the fertilised ovule in the flower. This single cell develops into the embryo within the seed. On germination the seedling plant begins its **juvenile** phase. Plants that are in their juvenile phase make vegetative growth and are unable to respond to flower-inducing stimuli. Over time the juvenility phase is lost and a transitional phase occurs before the **adult** or **mature** seed-producing phase occurs.

These phase changes are particularly obvious in some Junipers and especially in the wild English ivy, *Hedera helix*. On old ivy-covered trees the flowering stems of the ivy have quite different stems and leaves from the clinging stems and classical ivy-like leaves of the juvenile form (see Figure 26). The **senile** phase follows the adult phase.

juvenile leaf   adult leaf

Figure 26: Juvenile and adult forms of an ivy leaf

Horticulturally, from a propagator's point of view, the juvenile form of plants are the ones that root more easily. Adult wood of oak, apple and pear are very difficult to root.

It is possible to gain the benefits of juvenility from many adult phase woody plants by making hard pruning cuts – the resulting shoots may be much easier to root. Woody stock plants which are grown as hedges, i.e. with an annual routine of hard cutting back (and those other stock plants pruned hard similarly, if not grown as hedges) are able to produce much more cutting material which is much more uniform and much easier to root.

A further factor is the nature of the nursery trade. Plants which are the same genetically may be much more saleable in one or other phase, e.g. the feathery foliage of *Chamaecyparis* 'Ellwoodii', the intermediate foliage of *Chamaecyparis* 'Fletcheri', and the flat foliage of *Chamaecyparis* 'Alumii' – all of which are cultivars of *Chamaecyparis lawsoniana*.

THE SITE OF THE CUTTING ON THE STOCK PLANT

For stock plants grown as hedges the areas to avoid using as cutting material may be:

i)   those shoots below c.450mm from ground level, because of the greater risk of soil-borne fungal spores splashed up in rain.

ii)   the very top centre of the plant – which has the highest juvenility factor. These may be of poor quality – thin and disease prone.

The best cuttings in practice may come from the sides of the stock plant hedges. These may not be the most vigorous but they will have enough weight and substance to grow well. The shape of the plant in its subsequent growth should be typical of the parent plant. There can be an effect on the shape of the plant for some species, e.g. the conifer *Sequoia sempervirens* (the Coast Redwood) where horizontal shoots may produce plants showing horizontal growth and vertical shoots taken as the source of the cuttings grow into vertical plants (trees).

Within this 'Chapter' on the care of the stock plants it may be useful just to review by heading some of the main factors, some of which are mentioned earlier.

Juvenility
Recently discussed.

Hard Pruning Treatments
As in the hedges of stock plants.

Replacement of Stock Plants
To endeavour to keep the juvenility factor – cuttings from younger sources may have better rooting percentages.

Stock Plant Condition

Cutting wood taken from well-grown plants which have had a balanced nutrition may root much better than cuttings taken from soft sappy shoots relatively full of nitrogen, i.e. it is desirable to have a high level of carbohydrates (carbon to nitrogen level) within the cutting.

Light

A good balanced level of lighting is desirable. This may mean that shading - as in the Paraweb Shade Halls which restrict the light to 50% (or more depending upon the width of the gap between the plastic based strips of shading and wind protection mesh.)

Cutting Location

On the stock plant – recently mentioned.

Etiolation

Mentioned earlier – the system of clothing stock plants in darkness for some period, maybe of 7 to 10 days just prior to bud break – for lilac (*Syringa vulgaris*) cv's and *Cotinus coggygria* cv's. Blackout shading, for some days, prior to the collection of the cutting wood, may also assist in conditioning the leafy shoots and also improve rooting in difficult plants. This may be helpful to:

- increase the number of cuttings available
- improve rooting and increase root initials
- lead to greater extension growth and "caliper".

(Caliper – the diameter of the stem. It is an American term but it is used in the UK. We might use the term stem diameter or quote circumference measurements.)

Time of Year

Some plants will only produce suitable root/wood/shoot material at certain times of year without the provision of a different environment – light/daylength/temperature.

Location of the Stock Bed Nursery

It may be easier to import cuttings of chrysanthemums and carnations grown under benign long summer day conditions in South Africa, Malta or California.

PROPAGATION FACILITY

There are a number of basic systems:

i)   Rooted as hardwood cuttings in nursery lines out of doors – maybe through a black polythene mulch.

ii)   Rooted under milky film polytunnel houses or low tunnels.

iii)   Rooted in frames and covered with 'cold' glass with or without shade or (historically laths) or coir/rotelene/nicofence or other shade material.

iv)   Rooting under glass, covered with polythene (or in the open) with bottom heat or not.

Rooting with mist and bottom heat.

The use of tented mist.

The use of dewpoint cabinets.

The use of fog.

The use of tented fog.

The use of tented fog with mist.

v)   Garner bin systems useful to induce callus production.

vi)   Daylight extension systems which may be useful for leafy cuttings where, by using night break lighting for brief periods, the light can be manipulated to influence the phytochrome of long day and short day plants to stay vegetative and to root better.

Crop Production System

For example, with or without hormones/fungicides/powders or dips. Direct sticking into containers or the use of running lines. CRF (Controlled Release Fertiliser) supplements in the rooting media.

STAGE OF GROWTH

Traditions vary but the pattern of selection of the cutting wood is similar in most cases. The size of the cutting taken has an influence on the shape and thus quality of the final plant. In general larger cuttings are not the best for plant shape but with their greater level of food stores the reliability of rooting may be somewhat better.

The syllabus lists stem cuttings:

- Soft wood. This is where the wood is still very soft – not woody. These cuttings are usually all stem tips.

- Green wood. These are similar to soft wood cuttings in their shape and form but the growth of the stem tip has slowed. It is no longer so soft. These green wood cuttings need the same level of care as soft wood stem cuttings but they are more resilient in the face of environmental adversity, e.g. drought or stressful sunshine, because they have more stored food reserves and their tissues are not as tender, soft and fragile.

- Half ripe. These are also sometimes called semi-hard wood. These are still leafy stem cuttings, usually of the stem tip. The base of the cutting is conspicuously woody compared with the soft or green wood cuttings.

- Hard wood. The stems become drier, harder and really firm from around late October. The cuttings may be made from this material up to and immediately prior to the sap rising in the spring.

A simplistic pattern for a hardy shrub such as *Weigela florida*

	J	F	M	A	M	J	J	A	S	O	N	D
Soft wood stem cutting					▓							
Green wood stem cutting						▓	▓					
Semi-hard wood cutting								▓				
Hard wood cutting	▓	▓	▓								▓	▓

HANDLING THE CUTTING MATERIAL

Once the wood is cut off from the stock plant the opportunity to replace sap is lost. Fluids (H_2O) can only be absorbed through the cut surface at the base of the cutting (and any wounding cuts). This is a far from ideal circumstance because so many living cells will suffer from the flood of water damaging cells by diluting their osmotic pressure, some cells dying from prolonged lack of air and the chance of infection from water borne diseases is almost only a question of time. Hence every effort should be made to keep the material as turgid as possible:

- Harvest the cuttings when they are turgid in the early morning.
- Keep the cut wood out of the sun.
- It may be possible to use a cool box with an icepack. It can be useful to have the surfaces wet inside the box.
- Keep the material wrapped in polythene as far as possible.
- Transport the plant material gently to the propagation zone (or cold store).

A good bundle of leafy cutting wood is easier to keep turgid in a polybag than just one or two pieces of wood. The transpiration from the bundle of leaves quickly brings the relative humidity up to 100%. Do keep the material carefully labelled.

FREEDOM FROM PESTS AND DISEASES

Pests

The range of pests that may be perpetuated through the use of cuttings as the propagation method include:

- Aphids – as overwintering eggs of the Peach Potato aphid (*Myzus persicae*) or as adult greenfly. There are many species of aphids.
- Brown Scale (*Parthenolecanium corni*)
- Eelworm – chrysanthemum eelworm (*Aphelenioides ritzemabosi*)
- Red Spider Mite – glasshouse red spider mite (*Tetranychus urticae*)
- Glasshouse White Fly (*Trialeurodes vaporariorum*)

- Western Flower Thrip (*Frankliniella occidentalis*)
- Cutworms - e.g. Turnip moth (*Agrotis segetum*) - and the much more serious Mediterranean Climbing Cutworm (*Spodoptera littoralis*), a voracious eater of protected crops, including geraniums
- Vine weevil (*Otiorhynchus sulcatus*)

Fungal Diseases

- *Rhizoctinia* - Damping Off
- *Phytophthora* – Root Rot – collar rot
- *Pestalotiopsis*, *Monochaetia* and *Glomerella* - three blights of cuttings of camellia, rhododendron, heathers and conifers
- *Botrytis cinerea* - Grey Mould
- *Verticillium dahliae* - Wilts
- *Fusarium sp.* (*F. oxysporum* is a common form) - a wilt infection
- *Puccinia horiana* - Chrysanthemum White Rust

Bacterial Diseases

- *Pseudomonas syringae pv syringae* - a wilt disease on lilac
- *Erwinia amylovora* - Fireblight of sorbus
- *Agrobacterium* sp. - Crown Gall
- *Corynebacterium fasciens* - causes fasciation, the curious flattened stems of forsythia and some other shrubs – a wider host range.

The problems with bacterial infections are relatively fewer than for fungal infection.

Virus Infections

These have been named after the host plant in which it was first found, not withstanding the fact that the organism may do much more damage to plants of other species.

- Arabis mosaic virus (sometimes abbreviated to AMV) damages strawberry, raspberry and narcissus.

- Cucumber mosaic virus (CMV) is known to infect *Stellaria media* – Chickweed. This infection may be **symptomless** but the infected chickweed provides an overwintering host for the virus that an aphid **vector** could transmit to privet, honeysuckle and *Daphne*.

It is clearly very important that the propagator is aware of the problems that may be present in or on the stock plant.

It is fundamental to good gardening to use the best possible material for propagation and that diseased or pest infested wood should not be used – at least without treatment.

Routine rogueing the stock beds of plants expressing symptoms of virus or other particularly difficult infections is a wise policy.

Routine sprays with pesticides may help to control the infections to manageable proportions.

It is exceedingly difficult to control a virus. The avenues available include:
- Propagation from seed – viruses rarely infect seeds.
- Propagation from shoot tips which have been grown from specially forced growth of the stock plant. It seems that the virus particles do not grow and multiply as fast as the shoot so the very end tips of the newest growth may be free from virus infection.

TRUENESS TO TYPE

Plants may sport (deviate from type) – a mutation which usually occurs naturally. This is more correctly termed **bud sport**. A shoot or branch or flower, or just part of a flower or fruit, may develop differently from its parent.

We are familiar with russetted apples and smooth apples (red apples and green apples). The variety of the apple trees may be the same but the market value of the fruit may vary hugely. A 'Golden Delicious' apple with a corky, rough skin is curiously almost unsaleable - as may be a crimson 'Bramley' cooker. The customer expects smooth green apples in each case. Superb smooth, crimson striped with scarlet, forms of Cox's Orange Pippin (apples) do exist and there is a high market value for a new sport that has a greater sales potential.

Most of the varieties of chrysanthemum where they are in a series, like 'Bright Golden Princess Anne', the colour forms have come about as bud sports that have been noticed and propagated.

So it does matter that the cuttings are taken from known material (its **provenance**) and that the crop will come true to its clone.

A CLONE AND WHAT IT MEANS

A clone is a group of individual plants of uniform genetic constitution propagated from an original individual plant, by non-sexual multiplication alone, i.e. by cuttings, layering, division, budding or grafting (vegetative propagation).

The concept associated with the term clone is an important one for gardeners as many garden plants are propagated exclusively by vegetative means. These methods result in the creation of individual plants, all of which have the same hereditary constitution, derived from the same ancestor. Hence the importance of the initial selection – a plant with the best characteristics – of known entity.

The new plants are exactly the same kind of living matter as the one from which they were propagated and which they exactly resemble in all characters. (However, please see the earlier note on bud sports.)

If the plant is self-sterile then they will be sterile when crossed with one another. Hence a planting of individuals, all vegetatively derived from one seedling, therefore will all be members of the same clone and, as a result, they will be uniform in appearance and more predictable in performance than a planting of mixed seedlings.

From another viewpoint, unfortunately they will all have the same susceptibility to attack from the same insects and diseases.

True to Type

All the members of a clonal selection should be true to type, that is of similar shape, height, colour, form and habit. The retention of a clonal selection as a true form also requires the sharp eyes of the vegetative propagator, who will rogue out the variants should they occur - following sporting – (a plant that has varied from the normal - in leaf, shape, habit, flower). Sports have given horticulture a great percentage of our garden varieties.

THE IMPORTANCE OF PROVENANCE

[A note both in relation to seed and vegetative propagation]

In essence provenance means the place of origin. The colder the climate zone in which trees, say, are to be planted, the greater the difficulties of overwintering and the more limited are the range of varieties which will succeed.

Many foreign plant introductions have been collected from coastal areas and are not as hardy as populations of the same species growing in hinterland areas. Species raised from original material that is collected from colder zones, such as some *Eucalyptus* species, will give hardier material for planting with less risk of winter injury.

The term 'provenance' is also used to refer to the **origin** or original home of a particular population or strain.

Certain trees grow wild over vast tracts of the earth, but within that genus and species are local strains which have become adapted to growing in some region, which can be very localised in its geographical range. Different provenance of the same species may look similar and there is no outward difference in them, but they behave in variable ways when grown.

For example, Sitka Spruce is grown in Britain, Canada and the USA and the seed has often been imported for this purpose. In Britain it has been found that seed with a provenance in British Columbia grows well, but those raised from seed of a provenance in California do not. The Californian crop grows too slowly in Britain, its natural selection over millennia having adapted the form of the species to the warmer, more Mediterranean climate. The opposite is also true of using spruce seed with a provenance in North Alaska, as this also grows poorly in Britain because it is adapted to the long summer daylight hours and high temperatures over a short compressed season in the far north.

Provenance characteristics are passed on from one generation to another, so it is wise to know the origin of original stock, particularly in forestry, or if the grower is to use it in propagation in his nursery.

Botanical gardens keep records of the provenance of all their material. At Kew Gardens one can sometimes see the original plant a century or more old and from which maybe all the *Viburnum farreri* have been propagated.

Provenance means also that, in essence, separate races have developed in different regions that can vary greatly in frost hardiness, rates of growth, ultimate height, moisture stress resistance, and susceptibility to pests and diseases.

7. USE OF PROPAGATION EQUIPMENT

In the last section the review of the factors concerning rooting success included the use of the specialised equipment. The objective when using specialist equipment is to optimise rooting/germination potential.

With regard to seeds, the Seed Testing Stations have a range of procedures designed to give the seeds under test every chance of germination. It is the translation of these optimum germination procedures into effective production systems which the various items of equipment, like closed propagating cases, mist and fog units, intend to provide.

In the case of seed, to the list of essential provisions - warmth, moisture and oxygen and/or light - has to be added a suitable resting place so that the developing radicle can begin to supply the germinating seed with water, nutrients and anchorage. It is relatively easy to keep seeds:
- at the right temperature – but this does need care
- in light or darkness and day length
- to provide a medium to grow on
- to provide oxygen – as in air
- to provide abundant water – but the difficulty comes about in the provision of moisture rather than the circumstances where water is not just a thick water film around the medium forming the resting place, but has become a layer of water which in effect excludes free atmospheric oxygen.
- to provide freedom from diseases
- to provide freedom from pests
- to provide freedom from poisons.

MIST PROPAGATION

The idea behind the mist unit is that a spray of water produced as a mist will moisten the leaf surfaces of cuttings. In essence the seeds or cuttings placed under the mist should be provided with all the moisture they require.

The thin film of water produced is just right for keeping the foliage turgid, for reducing the water loss from foliage, and the cut surface at the base of the cutting (or the surface of a seed) is kept moist at all times but not to the exclusion of air – which is available for absorption and use by the plant tissues through the thin water films.

This green foliage material continues to photosynthesise, creating new sugars to feed the demand for wound healing tissue and the development of roots.

Seeds can absorb abundant water and expand without hindrance. The emergence of the radicle should be the most natural thing.

These circumstances are all fairly true in practice, but the mist unit does require attention to:
- reduce draughts
- ensure all the nozzles are working to provide a good coverage
- retain hygiene
- check mist sprays are working with sufficient frequency
- check temperature is even and up to the requirements (at the point where the seeds are to germinate and at the base of the cutting – the air temperature may be somewhat cooler)

Mist units work well but there are limitations and some difficulties. Possibly the greatest difficulty comes from the use of hard water. This inevitably dries on the plant material and for slow rooters a lime scale does occur. Mains water can include a huge range of chemicals other than water and a really good source of suitable water is desirable.

The water treatments with nitric acid may be hugely helpful in both softening the water and so reducing the quantity of carbonates but also in providing a hint of nutrients – nitrate which can be encouraging for seedlings and cuttings. The chlorine provided by the water companies may be helpful in reducing water-borne pathogens.

Mist propagation has become widely used in recent years, particularly on shrub nurseries for leafy cuttings (and occasionally for seed raising). Previously growers tried to prevent evaporation from their cuttings by keeping them in closed frames, which were kept shaded. With some cuttings where rooting is slow, shade is detrimental. Moreover, light is essential to growth and, up to a level equivalent to a cloudy day in March, the more light a plant gets the better it grows.

Cuttings kept for long periods in closed frames under conditions of high humidity tend to rot off. Hence the necessity for a method whereby transpiration is checked without the necessity for shading. It can be done by continuous overhead irrigation using fine nozzles, but this tends to supply too much water to the bed, which becomes over-wet even when the bed is heated, as it usually is with underground electric cables. The answer is a hot water or electrically heated bed, with controlled intermittent misting operated by an 'electronic leaf'.

The 'electronic leaf' which is generally in use at present, consists of two carbon electrodes sealed in a block of plastic material. When the surface of the plastic block is moist, the current passes between the electrodes which keeps an electromagnetic valve shut in the water supply. When the moisture evaporates from the 'leaf' (which replicates the evaporation from the leaves of the cuttings) the current is broken and the water supply is opened, to close again when the surface of the 'electronic leaf' is moistened. In practice this means that cuttings are kept constantly moist without too much water going on to the bed, which would happen if the 'mist' were continuous.

The frequency of applications is determined by the evaporation rate of the water film from the surface of the controlling 'leaf'. Spraying is thus regulated in accordance with the weather. When hot and dry, the misting may occur every ten minutes or so, whereas in dull weather and at night it may only occur every hour or less. The burst of mist should only last 1½ - 3 seconds.

Mist Equipment

There are several types of mist equipment available but they all benefit from a supply of bottom heat. This is supplied in a range of ways including cables or bare wires and a transformer, foil systems and heated waterbeds. Whilst the bed temperature is high, the house temperature may not need to be more than 10°C for many plants, 15°C for those which need warmer temperatures. To get maximum efficiency, a water pressure of 50lb per square inch is essential. Where pressures have to be operated below this, a booster pump is necessary. A water supply with a high lime content should be avoided if possible. Water authorities will not permit this type of installation to be connected directly to a mains supply and it is necessary to install a pump and pressurised reservoir with a supply tank fed by rain or tap water.

The bed itself should be about 150 – 200mm deep and constructed of rigid durable material. The base can be concrete, metal or rigid polystyrene and must have drainage holes. A 50mm layer of gravel is put in first, on which the soil warming cables are laid. The rooting medium is placed over these. Some shade in the summer is of benefit and frequently growers use a "tented" mist system with a polythene film, enabling them to use higher light levels than were possible with the closed case systems of the pre-mist days.

Examples of plants propagated under mist:
- Hydrangea 'Bluebird'
- Kerria japonica
- Philadelphus 'Avalanch'

Rooting Media

Experiments have been carried out at various centres and by individual growers and there are different opinions as to what is the best. Whatever is used it must be a free-draining material or the bed will become soaked and remain so.

A useful mixture consists of four parts coarse perlite or sand to one part peat. Some peat seems desirable, partly perhaps to create a more acid rooting medium, and especially for such plants as Rhododendrons and Ericas.

Whilst it is the common practice to root the cuttings into the bed, some growers use the bed as a plunging medium and strike the cuttings directly into pots or boxes. This eliminates the problem of having to move them when the cuttings have rooted. Most plants suffer during the move, as under conditions of mist few root hairs are produced, hence a weaning period is necessary.

At least one firm produced a 'weaner' that automatically reduces the amount of water falling on the rooted plants, thus allowing the change in regime to be carried out in controlled stages. If a 'weaner' is not used and the plants are struck in the bed itself, the change can, to some extent, be offset by placing the cuttings, when potted off, into a closed frame for a few days. Alternatively, protect them with a polythene overlay, after which they can be placed on the open benches.

Whilst cuttings may be inserted at almost any season of the year, better results are obtained by choosing the optimum time to take the cuttings. In no case should soft cuttings be allowed to wilt.

There are no absolutely hard and fast general rules for the time to take cuttings. However, it may be said that leafy soft wood stem cuttings benefit from the good light of spring and summer.

Cuttings of deciduous material rooted in the late summer and autumn may be difficult to overwinter if they shed their leaves.

Some evergreen shrubs and tree material will root in the early autumn much better than later in the year, e.g. Garrya, and some deciduous hard wood stem cutting material will root very well at the very end of the winter and just before the spring upward sap flow commences. (Once this starts there is little chance of rooting hard wood stem cuttings.)

Many books on plant propagation offer times for rooting species and cultivars.

Plant	Type of cutting	Season/Months for preparation
Begonia rex	Leaf	Spring, summer and autumn
Geranium	Soft wood stem	August to October March to May
Buddleja davidii	Soft wood tip	June, July
Buddleja (deciduous)	Half ripe and green wood	July, August
Buddleja	Hard wood	October to November, December
Viburnum davidii (evergreen)	Soft wood Half ripe Evergreen hard wood	June, July July, August October to late January

Table 5: Example of rooting times

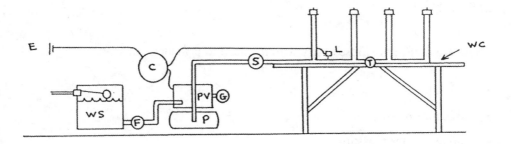

Figure 27: A mist bench diagram

Key:

WS = Water Supply (with float valve).
F = Filter.
E = Electricity supply.
C = Control box. This converts the electrical resistance signalled by the "leaf" into "on or off" power for the solenoid.
P = Pump.
PV = Pressure Valve.
G = Pressure gauge at between 2 bars and 4 bars.
S = Solenoid valve.
L = "Electronic Leaf" – a safe electrical device.
T = Thermostat.
WC = Warming cables.

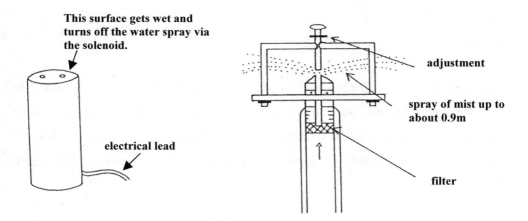

Figure 28: The 'electronic leaf'

Figure 29: A mist nozzle

FOG UNITS

These are noticeably more costly with the need to provide:

- very clean water
- high air pressure
- modest water pressure
- together with the temperature, light and draught conditions.

The idea of the fog is that there will be a continuous fog so that the plant material is surrounded by a totally damp environment with no opportunity for the foliage to suffer from water stress.

The fog system is excellent but does require attention to detail and monitoring in its operation to ensure that the sequence of emission of the fog is regular.

Examples of plants propagated under fog include:

- *Bougainvillea* 'Brilliance'
- *Camellia x williamsii*
- *Cestrum elegans*

The operation systems for fog vary considerably. An approach is to have relatively low water pressure, e.g. normal tap mains (if the water is suitable, i.e. soft water) and to eject this as a small spray at the nozzle. This is then hit by a massive blast of air that breaks up the water particles to form light as air fog particles. (See Figure 30.)

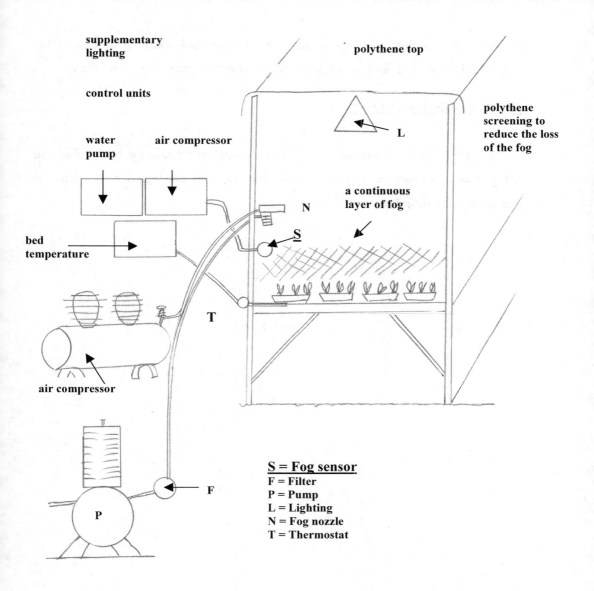

Figure 30: A fogging system

Well, one has to ask, is all this equipment necessary? What happens in nature? Is it all necessary? The answer really has to be yes, because in the case of softwood cuttings the plant (with a few exceptions such perhaps as *Salix fragilis*) would not normally be shedding cutting-sized stems or leaves as maybe.

In nature the number of seeds produced is colossal and wildly in excess of the number which are required in normal circumstances to replace the parent plant.

HEATED PROPAGATION

The way this syllabus is written is to go from the sophisticated to the basic. **The sun frame hut** - probably more important to our ancestral head gardeners - was the **heated propagating frame**.

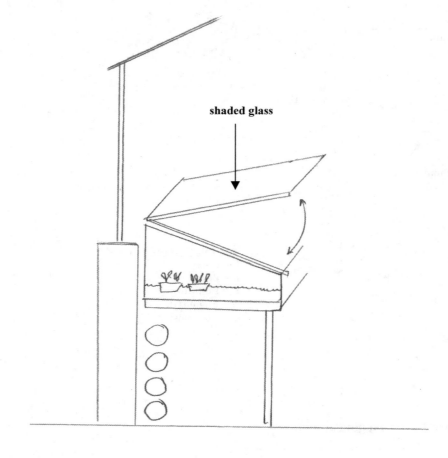

Figure 31: Heated propagating case

The closed heated propagating case was located over heating pipes. It was lined with moist peat and into this was plunged the pots, seed pans and trays of seeds and cuttings to be propagated. Inside the temperature was high – around 25°C, the humidity high and the light levels subdued. It remains a brilliant piece of equipment, but there are difficulties - particularly from fungi that thrive in warm, dank, humid conditions. Examples of plants raised in a heated case include:

- seeds of *Begonia semperflorens* Cultorum group
- leaf cuttings of African Violet – *Saintpaulia ionantha*
- stem cuttings of *Fuchsia magellanica*

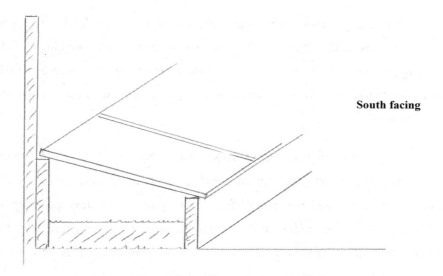

South facing

Figure 32: The sun frame

The **sun-frame** was located out of doors, usually facing south or south-west and backed by a wall or glasshouse.

The frame lights were heavily whitewashed and the cuttings inserted directly into the rooting media - loam to which a great quantity of coarse sand had been added so that the 'soil' drained superbly well.

It was very useful to root cuttings of *Anchusa, Statice* and *Phlox* and for stem cuttings of *Delphinium* and lupin at the start of the spring. These cuttings were watered heavily every day in the morning and again in the day if the sun had been very hot.

The traditional gardeners had some useful ploys as well. The use of a roll of laths (slender willow or poplar strips of wood available as a roller blind); coir matting on a roll was also available if the weather should suddenly produce a sustained level of massive sunshine, as can occur. Similarly, the mats would come out if the weather turned frosty, as again can happen in the capricious spring-time weather.

A revolution in propagation has come about with the use of **polythene** but this is not necessarily the end of the road. More evolution is still quite possible and every year propagators around the world are developing new techniques – most of which will have depended upon the understanding of the first principles upon which the plants' requirements depend.

An example of such experimentation has been undertaken at Oregon State University using sub-irrigation of stem cuttings as an alternative to mist. The cuttings were inserted into trays of perlite or pumice, the tray retaining water for 25mm of its 100mm depth. It is a simplistic system but somehow it had not been tried before, according to their research of the literature. The results were quite good – certainly good enough to be worth further development.

[Membership of the IPPS – the International Plant Propagators Society - is something that every professional plant propagator should consider.[1]]

---

[1] The current Hon Sec for the region of Great Britain and Ireland is The Secretary IPPS, Claire Shaddick, The Hurdles, Water St., Mere, Wilts BA12 6DZ – www.IPPS.ORG. Please note that it is modestly costly to join and only the dedicated pure-in-heart professional propagator should consider joining. That said the IPPS is one of the most wonderful societies – its motto is to seek and share.

Plastic Covers

Lightweight polythene sheeting has a very useful role in conserving humidity. Thus it may be used to create large units starting with whole tunnel houses and in various sizes down to the single pot in a polybag. The title may however be focused more precisely on the use of polythene touching the foliage of softwood cuttings. This is a useful technique. Water tends to condense on the polythene and this in turn keeps the surface of the leaves actually wet. In consequence the leaves are not under stress from water shortage from transpiration. The relative humidity is so high, there is little opportunity for water to escape from the leaves via transpiration or respiration.

The concern of the propagator quite rightly has always been that disease will establish and spread very speedily under such warm and humid conditions – so fertile for fungal growth.

Good hygiene conditions throughout the nursery area are an important part of the programme coupled with the regular use of fungicides. These (as at January 2002) include the active ingredients:

- Carbendazim (Bavistin) for *Botrytis* control

- Furalaxyl (Fongarid) for damping-off

- Furalaxyl (Fongarid) for *Phytophthora* and *Pythium*

- Furalaxyl (Fongarid) for soil or compost incorporation against *Pythium* and root diseases

- Fosetyl-Aluminium (Aliette) against *Phytophthora* in capillary benches, also other root rots.

These materials are not available on the amateur market and because the cost of a pack is considerable they are unlikely to be sold off the shelf. **As with all pesticides they require careful handling and proper procedures for health and safety**.

To what extent a candidate is expected to know about these products it is a job to guess, but suffice to say that the plant propagation industry would be vastly less successful were it not for the availability of fungicides to prevent the establishment and rapid progression of disease.

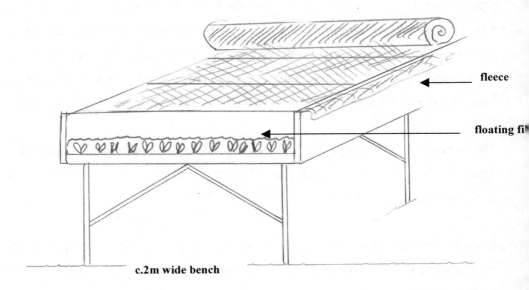

Figure 33 : The use of a floating film – a plastic cover used to help root a wide range of hardy ornamentals – in a raised bench with a fleece or heavier shading

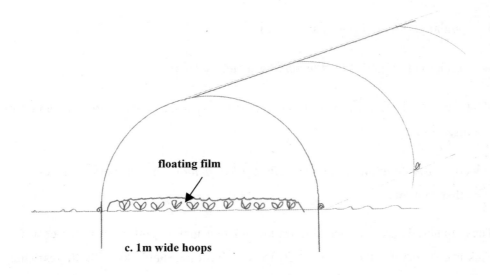

Figure 34: The use of a milky film low tunnel in the nursery field

Plants propagated under plastic covers may include:

- *Cotinus coggygria* 'Pink Champagne'
- *Kolkwitzia amabilis*
- *Nepeta grandiflora* 'Bramdean'

Heated Bins

The late Bob Garner of East Malling Research Station has been credited with the introduction of the heated bin as a system to encourage callus production.

Wound healing is encouraged by warmth – even temperatures of 10°C are much more stimulating than the outdoor winter temperatures. Cuttings taken in mid-November may not callus before mid-March – a long period for the open wound at the base of the cutting. This provides an opportunity for pathogens like stem rotting fungi to enter and generally reduces the rooting percentages as well as the overall quality of the growth in the nursery year.

There is much to be said for bundling the cuttings and inserting them in protected sites, such as in a frame surrounded by straw bales. The compost they are stood in should be of such a quality that it is never sticky wet – a very open gritty earth and some granulated peat might work well. An improvement again on the above is the **'Garner Bin'** – in essence a soil-warmed compost where the base of the cuttings are kept at c.20°C.

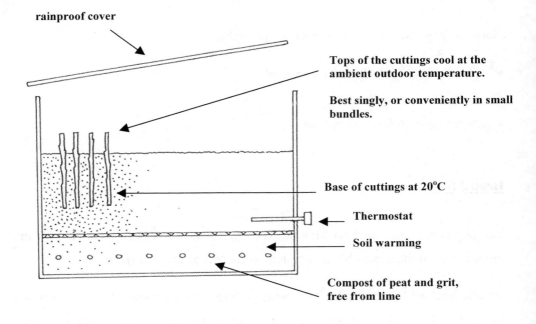

rainproof cover

Tops of the cuttings cool at the ambient outdoor temperature.

Best singly, or conveniently in small bundles.

Base of cuttings at 20°C

Thermostat

Soil warming

Compost of peat and grit, free from lime

Figure 35: A modified Garner bin

Bundled hardwood stem cuttings (approximately 20/25 to a bundle) may be "dunked" in fungicide and "dipped" in rooting hormone before being encouraged to callus, either outside "heeled in", or in protected conditions like a cold frame. Alternatively (as suggested earlier) they will callus more quickly, i.e. in about 2 – 4 weeks in a Garner Bin. In the normal way they should not dry out and nor should they be watered. It is a fine balance to get the compost moist but not "sticky wet" before "planting in" the cuttings about 24mm apart or in bundles, with care taken to ensure that all the bases of the cuttings are level and are in touch with the media in the bin.

Once the cuttings are callused, they can be put into "waiting" beds or frames to await the spring when the nursery site may be prepared to receive them. Callused cuttings are quite fragile and so for most soils it would not be ideal to push them into the rotovated earth (as is quite reasonable for a standard cutting) and then firmed. It is better to insert the cutting into a prepared hole and then firm it. A hazel stick "dibber" might do just fine. (Commercially, fine grooves are sometimes cut in the soil with discs.)

The pattern of taking the cutting follows the practices described earlier, cutting below a node or at the junction with older wood. It may then be dunked in a suitable fungicide to protect against the fungal infections present and dipped in hormone to stimulate callus. Wounding also may assist in achieving a large root system in the shortest possible time.

Examples of plants that may be propagated using a Garner Bin are:

- *Chaenomeles speciosa* 'Apple Blossom'
- *Rosa arvensis*
- Cherry rootstocks – *Prunus cerasus*

Dunemann Seedbeds

The use of leaf litter as a means of inoculating a seedbed with suitable fungi for mycorrhizal associations leads on to its consideration as a germinating medium for seed in the forest, woodland or thicket floor - the natural seedbed will be leaf litter and similar detritus. This idea may be stretched a stage further and in addition to providing the required fungal associations, further aspects of the natural environment may be stimulated to increase the successful establishment and development of seedlings.

The propagating conditions suitable for forest tree subjects could be provided by a reasonably deep layer of decomposing leaf mould overlaying a layer of sharp drainage material. At and after germination the entire seedbed would be shaded to reproduce the effect of the forest canopy.

Such a developed system was devised by Alfred Dunemann who patented a technique in Germany in the mid 1930's. The system was introduced to this country in the early 1950's and has found limited use for the production of coniferous subjects or forest tree nurseries.

Construction of Dunemann Seedbeds

The specification provides for the erection of the seedbeds using sideboards to a height of 35cm and 1 to 2m apart. The basal 10-15cm is filled with small weathered clinker that is levelled off with small grade ash. This provides the drainage layer. The frame is filled with leaf litter from the forest floor which is well firmed as it is added. This is finally levelled off at some 5cm from the top of the boards. This is topped off with sifted leaf mould. Dunemann specified particularly that the leaf litter should be a mixture of that provided by the Norway Spruce (*Picea abies*) and the Sitka Spruce (*Picea sitchensis*) and that the final sifting should be Beech (*Fagus sylvatica*).

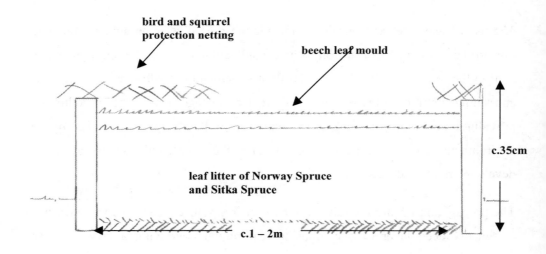

Figure 36 : Dunemann Seedbed

This illustration does not show the shading that is essential during germination - 50% shade achieved with 25mm wide laths spaced 25mm apart.

This system has proved an expensive item to produce and as might be expected has been modified in practice.

Experience has shown that alterations can be made to the system without detriment to crop production. Trials conducted over a wide variety of seedlings have shown that specific leaf moulds are not particularly advantageous and that virtually any coniferous litter will suffice. Observation also indicates that as long as a significant proportion (about half) of the litter is coniferous, extending it with other material such as hardwood leaf litter, peat or spent hops is not detrimental and may be a necessity if suitable coniferous material is not readily available. This then supposes that the major factor provided by the organic matter is purely physical condition.

Current information suggests that very many fungi will form mycorrhizal associations with one species of host, while one host will associate with many fungi on the same plant at the same time hence, as long as some inoculum is provided, the specificity of the source may not necessarily be significant.

The provision of sharp drainage has not proved an essential factor so long as the underlying soil has been well cultivated and is adequately drained. The depth of leaf litter has not proved critical and need not exceed 15-20cm for fibrous rooted subjects, such as most conifers.

This type of seedbed is potentially very useful for seed raising of:

- *Pinus sylvestris*
- *Calocedrus decurrens*
- *Taxus baccata*

Seed is sown and covered with a 5–10mm layer of sifted beech leaf mould. Water is applied <u>daily</u> during the germination period and until it is complete.

8. VEGETATIVE PROPAGATION

CUTTINGS

Taking cuttings is always a challenge because there are variables like the time of year, the quality of the cutting material and the technique available.

The types of cutting are based upon:

- stem cuttings
- leaf cuttings
- root cuttings.

Stem cuttings may be divided into:

- soft tip
- green wood
- half ripe
- hardwood

Within the softwood sector has to go the apical meristem cuttings and the surface sterilised larger propagules like the single rose eyes, frequently used now for roses in micropropagation. These specialised cuttings require clean laboratory facilities.

Creating illustrations for the three sorts of stem cutting is more challenging than to create (make) the cuttings in reality.

In the illustration (see below) drawn from a length of *Jasminium floridum* stem (this is an evergreen jasmine so the young stems look pretty similar year around) the condition of the wood coupled with the season (months) are the key to the type of cutting and its treatment.

- Hence a cutting at **A** might be too short and too soft.
- **B** might be quite okay.

- **B1**, the internodal cut, might be better because there is a short length of stem for anchorage.
- Cut at **C** and the lower leaf could be removed.
- **D** – similarly.
- A length of stem **A2** down to **G**, also **G1** down to **K**, would make fine green wood stem lengths for rooting – around July. The lower leaf would be removed.
- The length of stem **G1** to **L** would make a leaf cutting. The lower leaf would be removed.

Figure 37: *Jasminum floridum*   **Soft tip, green wood and semi-hardwood cuttings**

Cuttings bear the risk of a carry-over of pests and diseases so, as well as selecting true to type plant material, do also try to avoid scale insects, stem eelworm and canker to mention just three.

The size of the cutting matters. Very small cuttings may need more care than can be provided and too large a cutting may become desiccated due to lack of water. Virtually all the water has to enter through the cut base. Tradition is a useful guide for cutting size, plus the view that, in the first instance, if one gains a good root and a good shoot from a smaller cutting, a fine plant can be formed. Whereas a cutting just that bit too large may make a scrubby root system on a plant lacking vigour and with very poor, sparse branch framework which may never pick up to make the 100% standard.

The plant is made up of cells. The cells which divide are said to be **meristematic** and are most common in the **cambium** and at the **apical meristems** (in the growth buds and shoot tips).

The cut cells at the base of the stem of the cutting have several jobs:

i)   To try to stay alive.

ii)   To absorb water.

iii)   To multiply those of the cambium to heal the cut wound with callus tissue.

iv)   If possible to enable roots to form – both from the new callus and from root **primordia** already present in the stem tissues.

In order to stay alive the cells need water and oxygen, i.e. from the well-aerated and drained rooting compost. They must resist organisms of decay like the fungi. The absorption of water is not quite so easy to get right because the supply of water needs to be as a thin water film. Standing cuttings in water somehow tends to cause the cells at the bottom to die even though ample water may be absorbed to support the cutting for the time being.

In order to heal the wound, the cambium cells have to divide and produce additional cells that become the **callus** tissue. To encourage this cell division various steps can help:

i)   Select a suitable cutting size, in fresh 100% turgid condition and of juvenile material.

ii)   Dunking in fungicide helps to reduce the "load" of disease inoculum which may be present on the cutting.

iii)   An ideal rooting media mix – very low in soluble salt concentration (like the nutrients in manures and fertilisers) and yet supplying ample water film and oxygen in the "soil" air.

iv)   Suitable basal and air temperatures. It is the base of the cutting which needs the stimulation for cell division at this stage.

v)   Additional rooting hormones. The nuclei, which order the cells activities, are stimulated by naturally present hormones (**auxins**), fairly abundant at the nodes. The right strength of an additional rooting auxin may increase the rate of cell division and aid the development of roots.

Some rooting hormones are provided as a liquid, which may dry and leave only the hormone. Others carry the hormone in powdered talc. This generally works very well but if there is a thick layer, e.g. 1mm of moisture-laden talc, this may cut off some oxygen and reduce the speed at which the cell division is able to take place. Moulds may arise. Some rooting powders include a fungicide and this may also help to reduce losses. To counter the comments from some who may disdain the use of supplementary rooting hormones, one might suggest that, on average, since more cuttings will root and root better, i.e. more abundant and stronger roots are produced in the same time period, the extra work is well justified.

However, the pure minded 'non-chemical at any price' group are happy not to use hormones as rooting aids.

The hormone solution dips are based on dissolving the pure hormone in 'Meths' (Methyl alcohol) that is then diluted to 50% strength with water. The base of the cuttings only, just the cut surface, are allowed to stand in a shallow dish of this mix which then dries quite quickly from the cuttings leaving the hormones.

These treatments should in theory be the best because only the hormone should be left and just where they are needed. Also, they are very quick to do and can be completed in moments - no vast numbers of treated cuttings left standing, or dried out, for ages.

Twelve hour soaks in a much weaker hormone treatment have their advocates and the system is exceedingly good, but it does involve extra management so that the cuttings are looked after properly when they have completed their overnight soak.

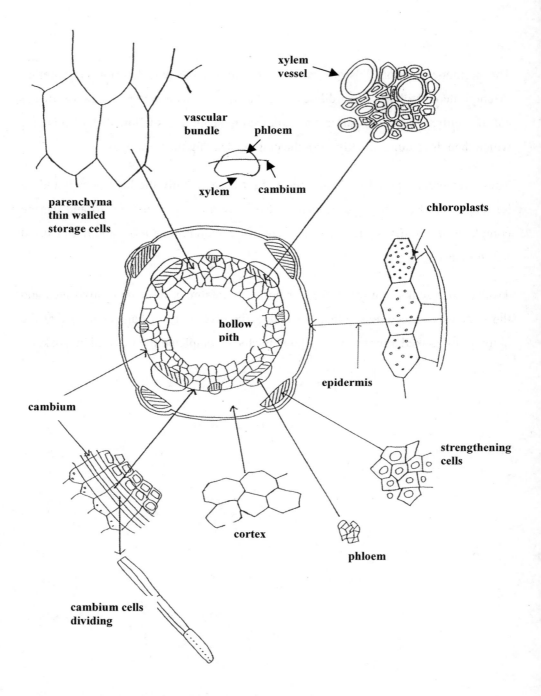

Figure 38: Cross section of young Lamium stem (much simplified)

xylem
vessel

vascular
bundle
phloem

xylem
cambium

parenchyma
thin walled
storage cells

chloroplasts

hollow
pith

epidermis

cambium

strengthening
cells

cortex

phloem

cambium cells
dividing

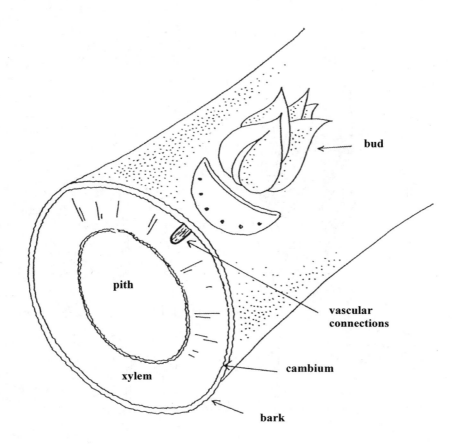

Figure 39: The base or bottom of a stem cutting

The origin of the roots may be from dormant root primordia present in the cortex –
easy to root subjects like some ribes and some willows may have these.

There are more methods than may be described here, but the principles are the same.
Attention to detail does matter and not every species roots easily from cuttings.
Alternative methods of propagation are usually used for "difficult" species – they are
usually seed raised, or grafted (or divided or layered).

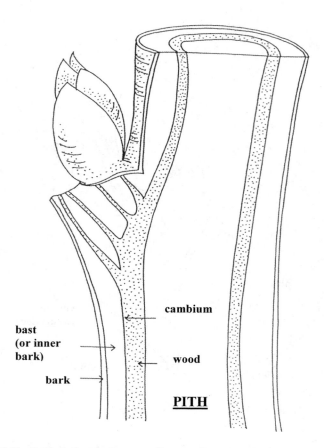

Figure 40: LS of stem tissue to reveal vascular connections

LEAFY STEM CUTTINGS (soft tip, e.g. shrubby plants)

Cuttings taken from lateral shoots of about 75mm – 125mm long which are not in bud, seed or flower are most likely to do well. Avoid taking cuttings from below 45cm above the soil surface to reduce the number of rain-splashed, soil-borne problems.

Cut the cutting off below a node or at a stem junction. This usually has the advantage of a solid cross section and more naturally present plant hormones.

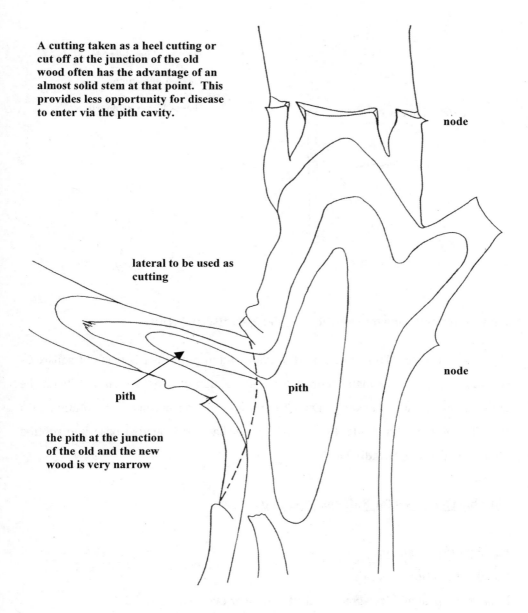

A cutting taken as a heel cutting or cut off at the junction of the old wood often has the advantage of an almost solid stem at that point. This provides less opportunity for disease to enter via the pith cavity.

node

lateral to be used as cutting

node

pith

pith

the pith at the junction of the old and the new wood is very narrow

Figure 41: *Salix fargesii* **sliced open to reveal the position of the pith**
(Cuttings taken at the heel may have very little pith)

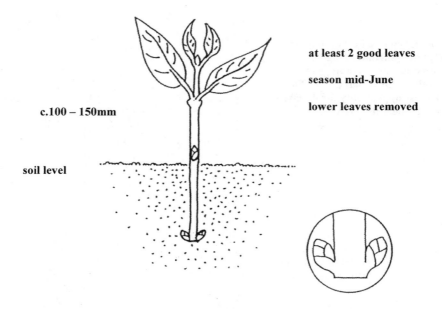

c.100 – 150mm

at least 2 good leaves

season mid-June

lower leaves removed

soil level

Figure 42: Soft tip stem cutting, e.g. *Weigela* **'Bristol Ruby'**

Cut below a node. This "flat cut" [for examination purposes] is best cut square as shown, but in practice many propagators cut through at a slant – cutting "with the grain" is easier and quicker. "Dunk" the whole of the cutting in a solution of a suitable approved fungicide, then "dip" the cut base or wounded base into rooting dip or powder, e.g. Seradix No.1.

Suitable Composts for Softwood Cuttings

Equal parts peat and grit
Equal parts peat and perlite
Equal parts peat and terragreen (a gritty granular clay-like material)
Equal parts grit and terragreen.

Temperature – for *Weigela* the optimum may be 23 – 25°C.
Relative Humidity (RH) – close to 100%, i.e. closed case or mist propagation or "fogging unit".
Light – long days (or night break lighting, i.e. supplementary to reduce the effect of long nights).

Level of illumination – ideal equivalent to a cloudy bright day. Some semi-opaque shade helps to reduce the stress of powerful sunshine when this comes.

Remove the lower leaves. Some leaves must remain to manufacture the sugars to enable growth and rooting to take place. Surplus leaves and those left in the compost tend to die off quickly and may set up *Botrytis* or other rots. Dunk the whole batch of cuttings into a suspension of a suitable fungicide plus a wetter (wetters include washing-up liquid). Use enough wetter to wet every part of the plant. (Among other virtues this treatment drowns many insects, but it doe not wet adult mealy bugs so they survive unless brushed off or moved). While still wet, dip the cut base of softwood cuttings into a rooting powder. Use enough – most of it seems to fall off when the cutting is inserted in the compost. Insert the cuttings into a mixture:

- which will support them
- is very low in soluble salts
- holds moisture
- is well aerated
- is comfortable for roots and root hairs.

In practical terms this often means equal parts of moss peat and perlite, or peat and vermiculite, or grit or peat and/or composted milled forest bark. For direct sticking (i.e. cuttings stuck directly into the pots from which they are to be sold) a compost of 2/3 prepared forest bark, 1/3 peat, with added slow-release fertiliser granules at the bottom of the pot before filling with compost may work very well. So if the pots held ½ litre and the rate of granules was to be $2kg/m^3$ then one would be using 2 grams per litre (1 gram per pot) - the weight of one "Smartie" (a popular chocolate confection).

Leafy cuttings need light, but not too much because this may cause excessive water shortage stress, a tension within the leaves, tending to close the stoma and this is counterproductive.

To counter this threat of stress in the height of summer under glass, one shade layer of Lobrene 30% shade is excellent or a single sheet of newspaper works well. (This should be removed for the winter batches of cuttings.)

Systems with fog, mist, polythene tents, closed cases, bottom heat and bell jars are all part of the heritage available to the propagator. Mist is as easy as any and tented mist (almost as in the Humex amateur mist propagator) is very successful in providing a high relative humidity. This keeps the cuttings turgid (and so stops them wilting) so that the leaves can assume their active function in the light and manufacture soluble carbohydrates (sugars) to transport to the wound healing/rooting zone which needs the sugars to provide energy.

Figure 43: A rooted *Daphne cneorum* greenwood cutting rooted in peat and sand under mist (Re-drawn from Montague Free)

Some de-leafing of senescent (old and drying leaves) and over-seeing may be highly desirable. Woolly plants do not like mist and not everything will root. Some tricky species really need to be prepared as cuttings at the mist bench itself, they seem to die so quickly, e.g. *Cotinus* and roses as softwood stem cuttings.

Rooting may take from a week to several months. If the water is limey then there is likely to be build-up of limescale on the cuttings under mist and this is undesirable. Rainwater may solve this problem though it is possible to acidify the mains water with nitric acid. This considerably benefits some species, especially the calcifuge group (lime-haters like heathers).

Under mist programmes once cuttings have rooted, some drying off from the very wet state is desirable to permit the development of root hairs.

Once cuttings have rooted potting off may be desirable into a loamless, peaty/bark mix plus ample feed for immediate growth and sustained nutritional resources. The ideal compost is stable, well-aerated, holds lots of water and nutrients and is free from pathogens. The John Innes potting mixes were often lower in their capacity for aeration and moisture holding when compared with the peat and forest bark and slow-release fertiliser mixes and FTE (the fritted trace elements which provide the micro-nutrients for the life of the compost).

HALF-RIPE CUTTINGS (sometimes called semi-hardwood cuttings)

These need treatment in virtually the same way as the softwood cuttings. They root more slowly and more reliably perhaps for the amateur with less than ideal facilities. The snag with deciduous material in particular is that if the young rooted plant fails to make adequate food storage within itself before winter and leaf fall, it may fail to grow out in the spring. The main season for half-ripe cuttings is in July and August.

The simple tented system below provides for all the principles and works well for the common species.

A system for the amateur (the technical would probably prefer to use a cutting compost like equal parts of moss peat and grit).

North side of bush in the shade.

Water the tray once thoroughly and drain before putting into the poly wrap.

Loosely wrapped clear polythene bag.

63mm deep tray well filled with cuttings.

Good garden earth – no fertilisers and no obvious slugs, snails, woodlice or millipedes.

not to scale

Figure 44: **Rooting semi-hardwood cuttings in a polythene bag outdoors**
e.g. for *Lonicera japonica*, *Hebe* 'Great Orme', *Deutzia compacta*

Hardwood Cuttings – Deciduous

These cuttings have their store of starch. They are best taken from juvenile wood, as would be produced by a hedge. Indeed many major propagators keep their stock plants in hedge forms because the system tends to produce large numbers of fairly uniform cuttings. These cuttings are low in nitrogen and high in carbon, as against the very dominant shoots, perhaps at the top of a young plant, which may have a higher nitrogen to carbon ratio and which root less readily. Ideal hardwood cutting material is 'fairly thin and hungry to grow'.

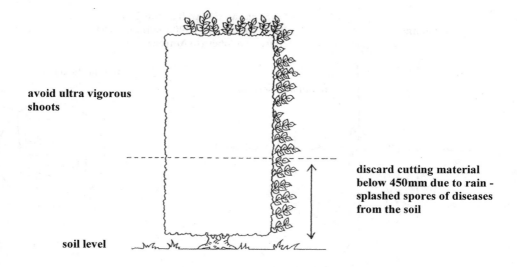

avoid ultra vigorous shoots

discard cutting material below 450mm due to rain - splashed spores of diseases from the soil

soil level

Figure 45: Stock plants for cutting material may be grown as hedges

The season for rooting ends when the sap begins to rise in the early spring – traditionally November is a very good time. For some species it may be better in October or even in early March just before the breaking of spring. It pays to keep a record of the treatments so that improvements may be aimed for as each season and crop of results is likely to vary and even tantalisingly good results may be difficult to repeat.

The principles involved are:

- to encourage wound healing and callus production
- to provide suitable rooting opportunities, i.e. ample oxygen and moisture in the compost
- to provide enough space for the subsequent plant development.

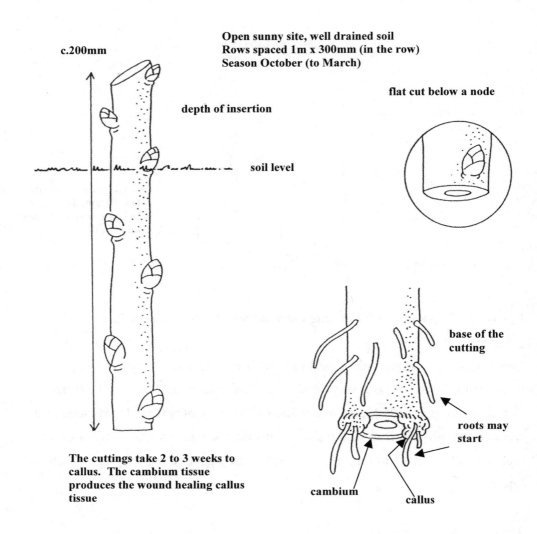

c.200mm

Open sunny site, well drained soil
Rows spaced 1m x 300mm (in the row)
Season October (to March)

flat cut below a node

depth of insertion

soil level

base of the
cutting

roots may
start

The cuttings take 2 to 3 weeks to
callus. The cambium tissue
produces the wound healing callus
tissue

cambium

callus

Figure 46: Traditional deciduous hardwood stem cuttings, e.g. *Ribes nigrum*

Useful but less usual types of hardwood stem cutting:

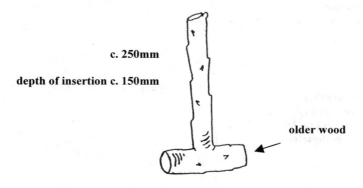

c. 250mm

depth of insertion c. 150mm

older wood

Figure 47:   **Mallet cutting, e.g. *Berberis stenophylla***

A mallet cutting really does work better for Berberis.

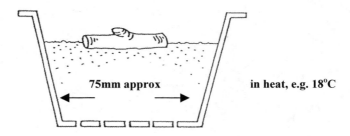

75mm approx   **in heat, e.g. 18°C**

Figure 48: Vine eye cutting, e.g. Black Hamburg

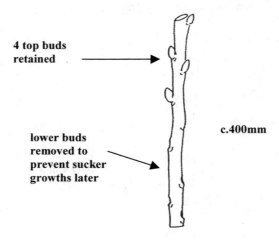

4 top buds retained →

c.400mm

lower buds removed to prevent sucker growths later →

Figure 49: Gooseberry or Redcurrant cutting for a bush grown on a 'leg'

HARDWOOD CUTTINGS – EVERGREEN

Treat as semi-hardwood, i.e. most cuttings would be quite small (102 – 152mm).

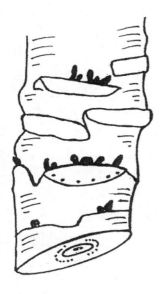

**Figure 50:
showing the basal buds at the
junction between the old and
the new wood**

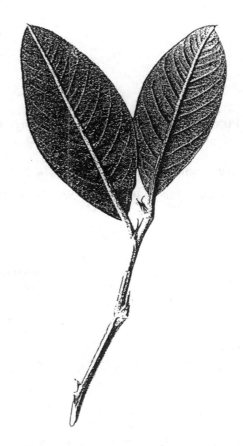

**this shows a clean slanting cut -
very acceptable in commercial
practice**

**Figure 51: an acceptable slanting cut
– square cuts are harder to do!**

A willow set (one of the very largest cuttings one is likely to encounter). These are usually planted where the tree is to grow.

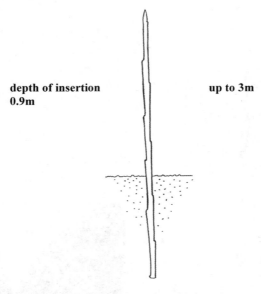

depth of insertion 0.9m   **up to 3m**

Figure 52: A willow set may be 3 metres or longer

Evergreen shrubs are often rooted as small hardwood stem cuttings under double polythene but without heat. Weed control by hand is desirable.

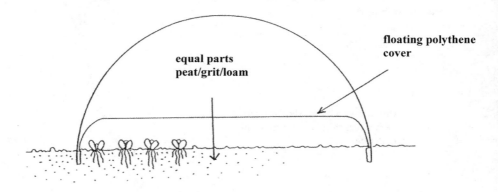

equal parts peat/grit/loam

floating polythene cover

Figure 53: Rooting evergreen shrubs under a double polythene cover

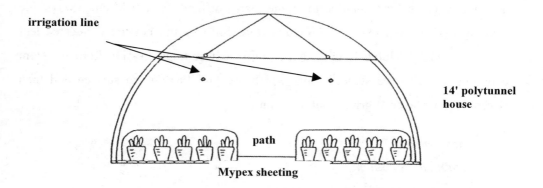

poly cover may be desirable up to mid March

irrigation line

14' polytunnel house

path

Mypex sheeting

Figure 54: 'Direct stick' evergreen or deciduous cuttings under double polythene

Regular fungicidal drenches may be helpful if there is any sign of *Botrytis* or other disease. The polythene sheet loosely covering the cuttings should come off by mid-April or so, to avoid overheating and the risk of disease infection posed by high temperatures, rapid growth and very high humidity.

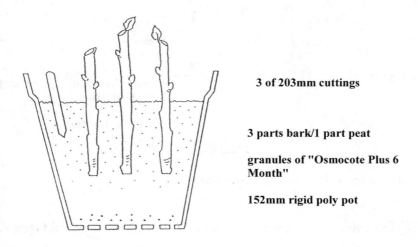

3 of 203mm cuttings

3 parts bark/1 part peat

granules of "Osmocote Plus 6 Month"

152mm rigid poly pot

Figure 55: Three cuttings in a container

ROOT CUTTINGS

This is a very useful technique for some plants difficult to root in other ways like Malling Crab C rootstocks, *Phlox paniculata* cultivars but not the variegated leaf forms like *Phlox* 'Norah Leigh'. N.B: phlox root cuttings are free from the stem eelworm. They have slender roots which are laid flat on the surface and then covered with a layer of grit (about 8-10mm).

> *Rhus typhina*
>
> *Limonium latifolium*
>
> The apple rootstock Malling crab C
>
> Species of *Pelargonium*
>
> *Papaver oritentalis*
>
> Seakale *(Crambe maritima)*
>
> *Anchusa azurea* 'Dropmore'

The root cuttings may be made in the autumn or the spring.

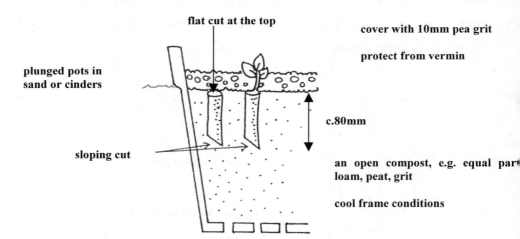

Figure 56: A root cutting system using a container

On a larger scale the cuttings are inserted in rows in the cold frame or tunnel house at spacings of c100 x 200mm.

Propagation by Root Buds

The great advantage of vegetative propagation is that the plants come true to type. (Exceptions may include the chimera sports, e.g. the variegated *Sansevieria trifasciata* var. *laurentii* which comes green from leaf cuttings, but is the true variety if grown from toes – the offsets.)

Figure 57: Raising variegated sports of *Sansevieria* from 'toes'

Most Yucca species may be propagated by root buds, e.g. *Yucca filamentosa*, also *Dracena draco* and *Cordyline indivisa*.

Almost in the same group of cuttings are the 'eyes' that can be cut from a stem tuber, e.g. potato. These will root and can be grown into good plants as a system to rapidly increase the stock of a special potato cultivar.

LEAF BUD CUTTINGS

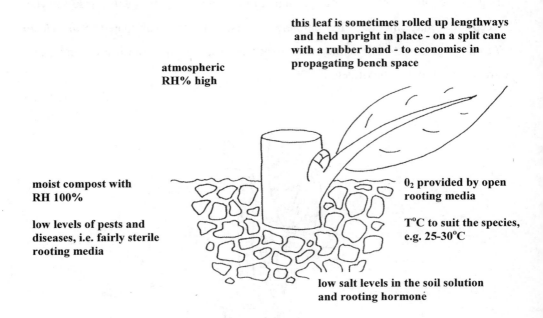

this leaf is sometimes rolled up lengthways
and held upright in place - on a split cane
with a rubber band - to economise in
propagating bench space

atmospheric
RH% high

moist compost with
RH 100%

low levels of pests and
diseases, i.e. fairly sterile
rooting media

O_2 provided by open
rooting media

T°C to suit the species,
e.g. 25-30°C

low salt levels in the soil solution
and rooting hormone

Figure 58 : Leaf bud cutting, e.g. *Ficus elastica*

Leaf bud cuttings are of use for a range of species including:

- *Mahonia japonica*
- *Camelia sinensis*
- *Rhododendron*
- *Rubus occidentalis* – the black raspberry
- *Rosa* species.

In essence the leaf bud cutting consists of a single leaf, the bud in its axil and a heel of the stem from which it was taken. It is very economical in material. The illustration of the *Ficus* shown earlier shows a short length of stem whole and in the round. In the case of other leaf bud cuttings the preparation of the cutting is more like that of a bud used for budding (shield bud grafting).

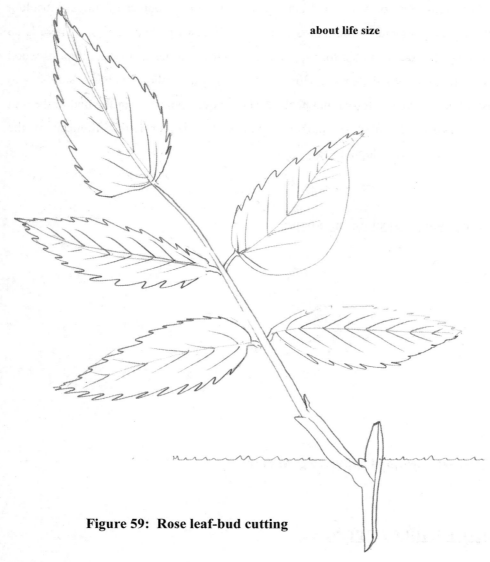

Figure 59: Rose leaf-bud cutting

- Temperature not too warm, e.g. 22°C.

- 100% RH (Relative Humidity).

- Rooting media 50/50 peat and perlite.

- Rooting hormones, e.g. Seradix No.2 0.3% IBA.

- A fungicidal drench, e.g. Filex.

- In open sheds.

- Under a clear floating polythene film.

This system relies on very clear cutting wood with few sources of fungal inoculum and a good fungicidal programme to prevent diseases getting control. There is so much cut surface available for infection and so much to heal. In the slither of wood there are mobile food sources. However, in this system photosynthesis is the key to providing the energy for wound healing, shoot development from the bud in the axil of the leaf, and root development stimulated by the hormones produced by the meristem in the developing shoot (tip).

An alternative system for 'insertion':

Figure 60: Leaf bud cutting, e.g. *Rosa* sp.

LEAF PETIOLE CUTTINGS

This is a useful technique for *Peperomia* and African Violet cuttings, also some *Begonia* cultivars and species. *Begonia rex* will root its petiole remarkably well but the plant that arises comes from the leaf blade (the lamina) from the hub point of the leaf veins which is where the petiole connects with the lamina.

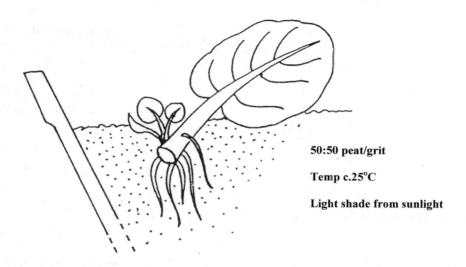

50:50 peat/grit

Temp c.25°C

Light shade from sunlight

Figure 61: Leaf petiole cutting, e.g. *Saintpaulia ionantha* 'Wedding Ring'

Alternatives: *Peperomia caperata* 'Variegata', *Begonia* 'Cleopatra'

LEAF LAMINA CUTTINGS

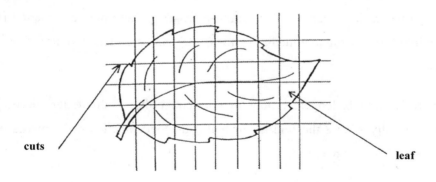

cuts

leaf

Figure 62: Leaf lamina cuttings, *Begonia rex*

Cut up the leaf into large stamp-like pieces, arise and lay or embed them vertically on the surface of a rooting compost, e.g. 50/50 grit/peat, 100% RH, temperature c.25°C, light shade or mist.

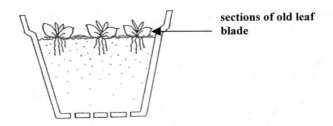

sections of old leaf blade

Figure 63: Plantlets of *Begonia rex*

Peperomia caperata 'Variegata' will also propagate easily by "diced-up" small leaf squares but not all the progeny may be variegated. *Peperomia argyreia* on the other hand would produce an all-true progeny. *Peperomia obtusifolia* Magnoliifolia Group may not be suitable for lamina cuttings but its propagation would be easily effected from stem cuttings.

Streptocarpus cultivars and species seem to come easily from leaf sections. Mature, whole, long, strap-shaped leaves are removed carefully from the stock plant and these may be cut into sections of c.60mm in length. These may be inserted right way up into trays of suitable media (as for *B. rex*) and plantlets will arise from the cut base.

Alternatively, slightly longer sections may be cut further to divide the pieces into two by carefully slicing the mid-rib in half. In good practice these pieces each produce short rows of plantlets.

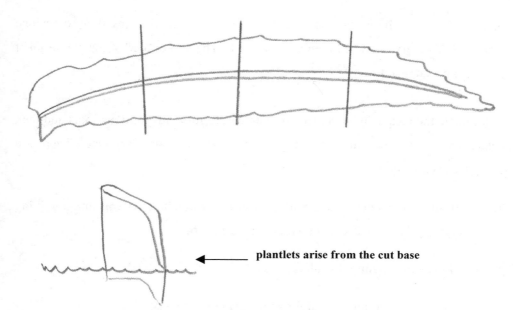

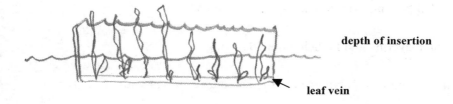

plantlets arise from the cut base

Half-section of *Streptocarpus* leaf

depth of insertion

leaf vein

Figure 64: Illustration of *Streptocarpus* leaf cuttings

A whole row of fairly uniform plantlets is the objective.

LAYERING AND STOOLING

Layering

Layering has distinct advantages and also considerable drawbacks. The great advantages are that the material is true-to-type and no special facilities are called for. Some very difficult plants will root.

The disadvantages lie in the awkward shape of the plants, the long time to achieve plants and the very restricted number produced. The appearance of the parent plant may also be damaged.

In principle the idea is to get a piece of the plant to form adventitious roots and then detach the rooted piece and encourage it to grow on its own account. There are seven basic techniques:

a)   Simple layering (or traditional layering) by wounding systems and involving burying the wounded stem which may then root.

b)   Tip layers – mainly for rubus species.

c)   Serpentine layering, useful for some clematis and wisteria.

d)   Dropping, where a plant like heather is deliberately planted too deeply.

e)   Stooled layering – mainly used for root stocks.

f)   Mound layering and French mound layering.

g)   Air layering with polythene or as a marcottage system with two half pots.

In general practice, **air layering** is the least successful due to the practical problems involved, but it is helpful for stove glasshouse species where rooting times are relatively short. The principles involved include:

1. That wounded or etiolated material produces adventitious roots if the occasion permits.

2. Layers are usually done prior to the main periods of rooting out, i.e. in the spring or the early autumn (though some species root easily in the summer).

3. The size of the piece to be cut off should not be excessive or the few roots will not be sufficient for independent survival.

a) Simple Layering

This can be carried out throughout the year if there is suitable wood present. The optimum times may be August/September/October/November and April/May.

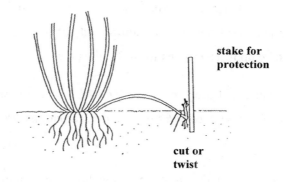

Twisting the stem immediately prior to the layering insertion operation is probably as good and is certainly less risky than cutting because it is very easy to break off the piece to be layered while pegging down and earthing up.

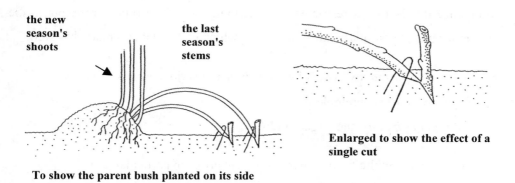

Figure 65: Simple shrub layering, e.g. *Rubus tridel*

In more productive systems using simple layering, the stock plants are maintained in a nursery bed and cut back to obtain long vigorous shoots. The plant is then lifted and may be planted on its side.

This has the advantage that more branches are close to the ground and hence much easier to layer. Some sort of wound is made in the selected stem, e.g. cutting upward for 51mm or so through a node to form a tongue. Removal of ring of cortex or, most commonly, by wrenching the stem to break the tissues. The wound is often treated with rooting hormone powder and the stem pegged down into prepared soil. The operation is carried out at two main periods of the year, April and September. Rooting may take up to 18 months for difficult subjects.

Examples of plants that are layered include *Magnolia grandiflora*, *Chimonanthus virginicus* and *Eucryphia cordifolia*. Border carnations are frequently layered in July/August.

A very much more efficient use of the simple layering system is described under the paragraph e) **stooled layers** and f) **French mound layering**. The **serpentine layering** in paragraph c) works for some species, e.g. *Hydrangea serratifolia*, *Hedera canariensis*, *Vitis coignetiae* and *Vinca major* 'Variegata', but it does produce awkwardly shaped plants.

b) Tip Layers

In practice this is almost restricted to some members of the rubus group but in the garden we may be familiar with some weeds which can tip layer remarkably well:

- *Rubus cockburnianus* (which I would class as a serious weed)
- *Rubus fruticosus* – bramble
- *Calystegia sepium* – the larger bindweed

Brilliant in their simplicity for *rubus* and loganberries in particular.

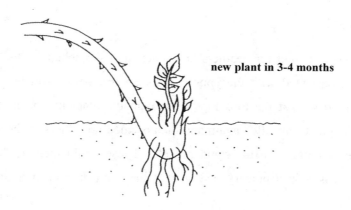

new plant in 3-4 months

Figure 66: Tip layering

Bury the growing point and this swells, develops roots and creates a crown with a shoot. By pinching back the early shoots on the stock plant it is possible to develop quite a number of extra stems enabling useful numbers of plants to be raised in this way, e.g. 16 to 20 plants per stock plant should be a fair target for production.

c) Serpentine Layers

Rather like the image of a Loch Ness monster. Ground level shoots of vines, wisteria and clematis may be wounded, pegged down and earthed up to produce, hopefully, a "chain of layers".

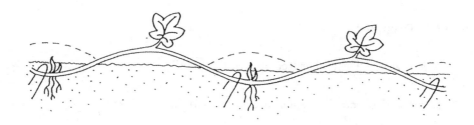

Figure 67: Serpentine layering

These may be quite difficult to root, although in principle they are easy to do.

d) Dropping

A very easy method for heathers and other multi-branched plants. The plants are lifted and replanted with the young stems set just below soil level and fine earth intermingled so that the tops look as though the plant has been stooled. After a season the plants are lifted again and then divided up – most of the shoots will have developed enough root to "stand alone". These could then be "lined out" for a growing season in a nursery bed so that they can develop a good well-furnished shape.

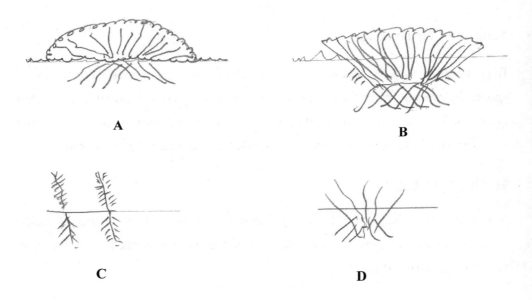

A

B

C

D

Figure 68: Dropping

A   *Erica carnea* 'December Red' growing normally

B   Lifted and 'dropped' – replanting it c.70 – 100mm deeper

C   After lifting for the second time at the end of a growing season – rooted branches may be harvested and lined out

D   Sometimes, for precious plants, it may be worth saving the stock plant for further use after recovery

e) Stooling

This is a very important production system. Quite a number of woody species – *Tilea, Corylus, Malus, Pyrus* – will "stool". That is when they are cut back almost to ground level they will regrow vigorously with a 'ring' of young stems. If these developing shoots are earthed-up in the dark moist earth, the base of the shoots are softer (etiolated) and root readily. At the end of the growing season the earth is drawn away leaving the rooted stems to be harvested, to be lined out in the nursery for use as plants in their own right, or for budding in the following season.

It is important that the nursery soil is very good for this purpose in order to get the good quality growth – in length and caliper (stem diameter).

In the creation of the stool bed a batch of layers is lined out with ample space between the rows, e.g. 2m, to permit mechanical cultivation and supply the earth for the earthing-up. Organic matter, extra soil nutrition and irrigation are all valuable aids to achieving a good nursery season of abundant rooted layers well up to the standard required.

Production numbers of layers in Europe may be high and measured in 100,000's per species/cultivar.

In the second autumn the stooled layers are harvested, graded and lined out in the nursery for working (budding) the following summer.

Wood chips, thought at first sight an unlikely medium for rooting into, in fact are used to excellent effect in the USA. They are very clean, easy to move with blades or blowers, they filter in between the young shoots well, they are well aerated and there seem to be no nutritional or pathogen problems. The difficulties with earth can relate to texture and mud-like properties when wet and the difficulty of wetting very dry mounds when the need is great.

a) Lined out layers to make
the stool bed

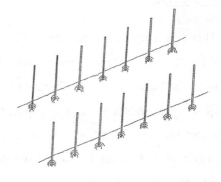

b) Cut back to ground level
in the first winter

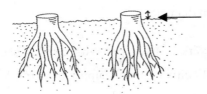

c.20mm

c.2m between the rows

c) Sequential earthing up during the
growing season as the shoots grow,
so they are earthed up

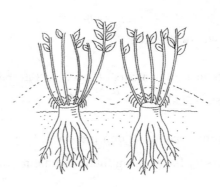

d) At the end of the autumn the earth is
removed, the rooted layers are cut off –
harvested for use – to be lined out for
budding in the summer

Figure 69: Stooled layers

f) Mound Layering

This is another etiolation layering system and it can be very helpful for the *Cotinus coggygria* group which are reluctant or very difficult under mist.

Branches of the stock plant are spread-eagled on to the soil and then pegged flat on or just below the soil surface. Shoots may break out along the length of these branches and as they grow, these are "earthed up" several times. It is not unusual for the whole of the stock plant to be pegged out flat and enough new shoots from the central area develop each year to permit the continuation of layer production each year for many years.

French Mound Layering System

The French system whereby the branches are pegged into shallow trenches is much more labour intensive. It is astonishingly hard to do single handed – the stems rarely seem to fit the shallow trench provided and in particular may be so springy that the peg system is tested to the limit! Just to grow them on the surface seems to work well – in a nursery system provided there is extra compost available to earth up the young shoots as they grow along the stems.

g) Air Layering

This has its place as a technique but it is very rarely practised. Its role may be for the propagation of some ancient plant that is so old and precious that it cannot be moved or cut back to produce new shoots for cuttings or layering at soil level.

In essence the stem is usually wounded at a node near to the growing point, e.g. 100 – 150mm from the tip. This wound may be treated with hormone powder. It may be that the wound, if a cut, could be wedged open with a small piece of sphagnum peat. Around the node more moist peat is wrapped and the whole poultice is covered in black or opaque polythene.

The process can be done year around with a routine of inspections to check that the peat is moist and for rooting. If and when a good root system is present – the air layer may be detached and grown on with nursery care because the roots will have much development to achieve especially in the early days following its detachment.

Marcottage

This ancient practice is worth a mention – it has a role. Two half pots are used instead of the polythene. Its role today may be very rare indeed but it can be used to reduce the height of valuable *Dracena* or *Ficus* or *Monstera* trees in conservatories.

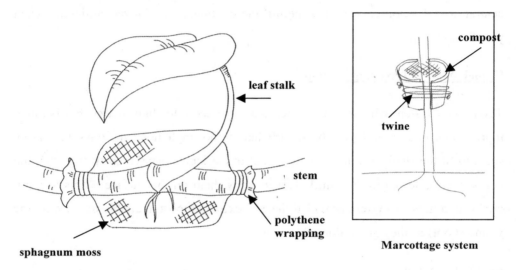

Figure 70: Air layer of *Epipremnum aureum* (Scindapsus)

No wounding may be required with this method.

Natural Methods of Propagation:

RUNNERS AND STOLONS

Runners are specialised structures, developing first as stems from the axils of the leaves of rosetted plants. These stems produce new plants.

Examples are in violets, *Saxifraga sarmentosa* and strawberries. Stolons are similar, i.e. stems rooting at the nodes where they touch the soil surface.

Offsets

These resemble runners and originate in the same way, but are shorter and stouter. One offset will produce only one young plant. A dome-shaped plant is produced. Examples include *Sempervivum tectorum* and many *Saxifraga* and other alpines.

Runners

Strawberries are propagated by runners. These are naturally produced, surface growing stems which develop rapidly from the crown of the parent plant from around early July.

With strawberries the importance of healthy stock is paramount if the plants are to have a reasonably long and heavy cropping life. Virus infections, including Yellow Edge, Severe Crinkle and Green Petal are all potential problems, as may be Red Core – a fungus disease (a wilt infection), *Verticillium* wilt, which is also a fungal infection.

A general symptom of infection, visible from a distance, is that the crown of 'sick' strawberries is flat. Stunted, low plants are an indication of a problem – which might only be due to waterlogging or other poor soil conditions, but strawberry plants should only be propagated from very healthy plants which have a good cropping history.

Commercial growers use Certified Stock, that is strawberry runners grown in isolation and which have been inspected to establish that they are true-to-type and free from known virus infections.

Strawberry Runner Production – Isolated Blocks

An example of a system of growing the stock plants in 2 metre squares:

At planting   **In early July**

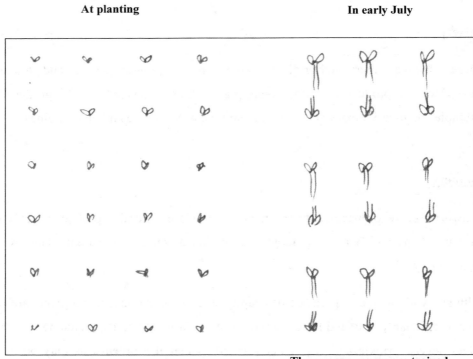

**The young runners are trained
towards each other**

**By early
September
the
abundant
runners are
trained into
isolated
blocks of 4
parent
plants**

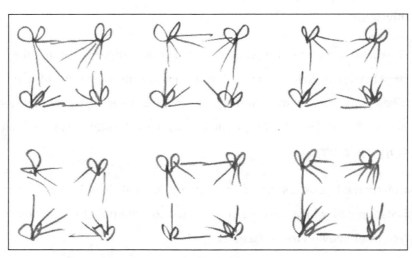

Figure 71: Strawberry production in isolated blocks

In the above system of isolated blocks, if there is a hint of infection the removal of an isolated block is relatively easy and any virus infection should have been confined within the four parent plants.

The runners may be pegged down to encourage the development of roots. Pot-grown runners, where the runner was pegged into a plunged pot filled with good potting media prepared to receive the runner, was a good system for the production of strong plants to grow to crop well in their maiden (first) year. There may still be a role for the pot runner.

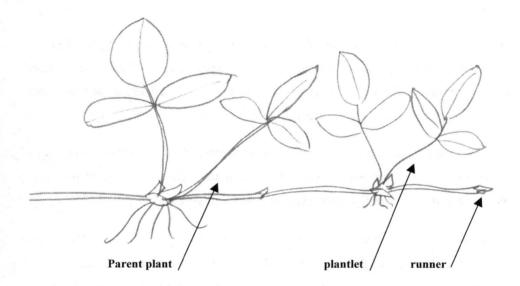

Parent plant   **plantlet**   **runner**

Figure 72: Strawberry runner

Strawberry runners produce young plantlets, already rooted, which may be detached from the parent plant or indeed removed prior to rooting and taken as cuttings. This has the convenience of control in a propagating environment (composts, nutrition, irrigation). From the runner, the growing point, forms a terminal bud which becomes the new rosette – the growth is then continued by a lateral bud.

In the case of a creeper like Ground ivy (*Glechoma hederacea*) or *Lysimachia nummularia* (Creeping Jenny), the plantlets arise at the nodes and the terminal bud continues.

DIVISION

This is mostly carried out on plants that produce an extending herbaceous rootstock. Some shrubs, such as *Kerria japonica, Mahonia aquifolium* and bamboos, may also be divided. Most plants can be divided at any time during the dormant period when the soil is not too wet or frozen. Others, such as *Scabious*, are best left until spring and some are better propagated immediately after flowering. Each divided portion should have roots and at least one growing point. The new plant should be selected from the younger outer portion of the plant, which is generally healthier and more vigorous.

Division has a role for a number of plants like the over-large 'seed' potato tubers that may be cut into portions. Many herbaceous perennials like Michaelmas daisies respond to regular division – the younger portions are retained and usually the inner older parts of the clump are discarded.

Nurseries often maintain their magnificent herbaceous fields by annual division and rotation of the crop around the site. This helps to retain the vigour of the young plant and it also ensures that each plant has plenty of space.

The classical technique for division is with 2 garden forks back to back. This retains more of the fibrous root than space or knife cuts. This is a useful technique and can be put into practice in the border in the late autumn, winter or spring renovation programme.

On a nursery scale the plants are lifted, taken to be split and then lined out. With some million plants to be produced on the larger nursery, the operation is phased around the weather – lifting – shed storage – splitting (with a knife and carefully pulling apart) – storage – lining out in the spring. The weather is rarely kind enough to permit the even sequence of operations without some storage periods.

The key issues of health and labelling – trueness-to-type – all have to be ensured throughout with good rogueing in the field, quality labelling and very reliable bin systems to keep similar-looking plants separate.

Each division should consist of one or more dormant buds and some roots. With evergreen perennials such as *Liriope* and *Carex* the leaves may be reduced by half to reduce transpiration.

Plants that have tuberous roots such as *Bergenia* can be increased by cutting up the **rhizome** into sections approximately 35mm long, each having a dormant growth bud, and placing in a mist propagator to encourage growth.

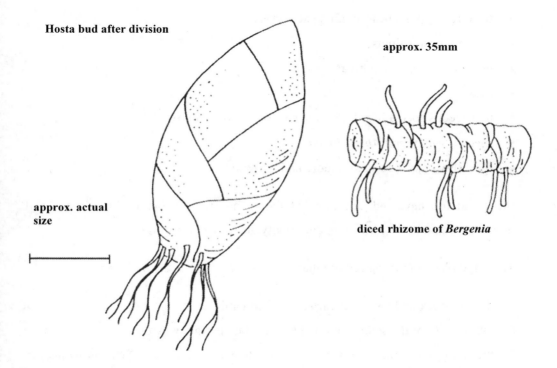

Hosta bud after division

approx. 35mm

approx. actual size

diced rhizome of *Bergenia*

Figure 73: *Hosta* division

Figure 74: *Bergenia* division (using rhizome as a type of stem cutting)

GRAFTING AND BUDDING

Budding is a particular form of grafting and uses just a single bud of the chosen variety to be grown.

Grafting is the union of 2 plants, one provides the rootstock and the other the aerial growth which is the recognisable rose or fruit tree. It is popular with nurserymen as a technique to produce uniform batches of plants which are difficult to root as cuttings. These include:

- fruit trees: apple, pear, plum, peach, cherry
- the very best walnuts
- the *Acer palmatum* cultivar
- roses
- herbaceous specialities like some paenoies, gypsophila
- speciality conifers: *Abies, Picea*
- speciality oaks, beech, sycamore and wisteria.

(Mist and fog have reduced some of the propagation problems for clematis and rhododendron that are now more commonly grown from cuttings.)

The principles of grafting require that:

1) the rootstock and the scion variety are compatible;
2) the polarity of the scion is correct (it must be the right way up);
3) the union takes place between the meristematic tissues and there is wounding necessary to achieve this;
4) the contact between the 2 cambium layers must be close and secure.

In practice, for dormant scion grafting, the scions must be fully dormant though the stock can be growing. (Frequently rather 'dry' rootstocks are preferred to reduce the flow of excess sap and also, in the case of conifers, resin as this excess juice may reduce the percentage 'take'.)

The Composite Tree or Bush

The production of a new grafted plant requires organisation - the provision of the rootstocks and the collection and preparation of the scion wood.

In the case of apples, the rootstocks are crab apples. (These were sorted out into clones with names by the East Malling Research Station in Kent and then became the Malling Rootstocks, such as MI. More recently, in conjunction with the John Innes Institute then at Merton, a new series was produced – the Malling Merton Series, the MM rootstocks – most of which have resistance to the woolly aphid pest bred into them from the crab apple parent crossed with an apple 'Northern Spy'.

The apple rootstocks themselves would usually be raised in stool beds as described earlier. The nursery lines would permit access for machinery and good growth so a suitable planting space arrangement would be 600mm between the stocks in the row and 1500mm between the rows. These rootstocks would be planted out before or during the spring of the year they were to be budded.

Budding takes place around early July. 'Chip' budding is more popular for fruit trees because it may be quicker and more reliable. 'T' budding, where the bud is slid under the bark of the rootstock via a 'T'–shaped cut, is still popular for rose budding. Inverted 'T' budding is possibly more successful because any disease spores which wash in the cut may tend to drain out.

In the nursery field the rootstocks are grown well to be clean and free from pests or diseases. The lower part of the young stem is kept straight and clean of side shoots because the chip bud will be inserted at maybe 300mm above ground level. This confers a benefit in that collar rot (an infection of the graft union) in later years is much less likely where the union is above soil level.

The scion wood is collected – ideally at dawn so that the material is fully turgid. It is kept out of the sun in a moist polybag. Only true-to-type, healthy 'bud-wood' should be selected. These are the young stems of the chosen apple variety.

What is selected is what will grow (hopefully!) and so it is essential that the stock plants offer the very best apple colour forms and other qualities like less russet than may be found in other sources of bud wood of the same variety. The bud sticks are de-leafed to leave a short length of petiole as a handle, but this is not essential.

In the field, the propagator may first make the cuts on the rootstock. The choice may be to use the north side of the rootstock so that there is less drying from the sunshine. Two cuts are made so that a chip of the rootstock is removed. This is then discarded and in its place is inserted a similar-sized chip of scion wood containing a growth bud. This is then tied in securely without delay.

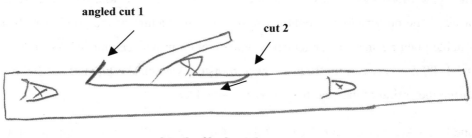

a length of bud wood

On the rootstock the chip bud is able to sit comfortably in the angle of the wedge-shaped cut. It is then tied in, most usually with a rubber tie strip or 'bandage'.

What happens next is the rootstock heals its wounds with callus tissue. The chip bud is able to stay alive because it has not dried out and its cut tissues are closely pressed against the similarly cut rootstock, so its cambium also produces some callus tissue. The competent grafter has prepared the chip bud and the cuts on the scion so that as much of the cambium tissue from the stock and the scion is exactly opposite each other. The new parenchyma cells of the callus intermingle and the chip bud is able to develop as a part of the rootstock.

Occasionally the buds grow out in the same summer, but more usually they stay fat and healthy. The bud ties are removed after a few weeks.

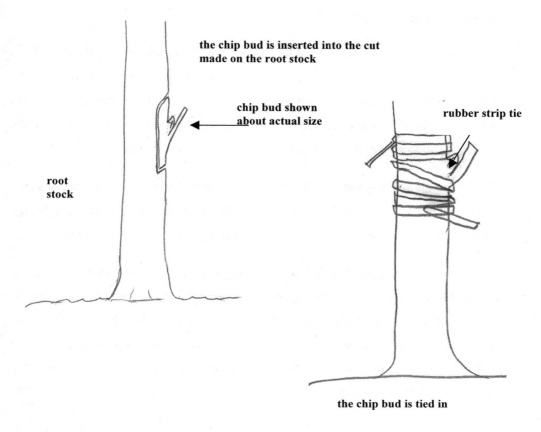

the chip bud is inserted into the cut
made on the root stock

chip bud shown
about actual size

rubber strip tie

root
stock

the chip bud is tied in

Figure 75: Apple chip budding

At the end of the winter the budded rootstocks that have 'taken' are headed back about 100mm above the 'bud'. This is to help in the production of a straight stem – the young shoot may be tied neatly back to this for the first few weeks of its rapid growth in the forthcoming growing season.

The new composite plant, consisting of the rootstock and the chosen scion variety, continue in the nursery for their maiden (first) year. The skilful nurseryman may seek to encourage branching at a suitable height so that on planting there is already the foundation framework for very strong branches.

Whip and Tongue Grafting

There may be some of the budded rootstocks that fail to take and at the end of the winter there is a second chance to get them to produce a maiden tree of equal quality to the chip budded trees. This is possible by 'whip and tongue' grafting. The whip is the name for the longer cut and the tongue is a device to help the scion sit on the cut of the rootstock. It also increases the area of cambium contact.

To prepare the scion wood it firstly has to be collected around December/January – clean young wood. This is bundled and may be stored partially buried upright in a damp north-facing border. In this way it stays ready for use for some months.

The rootstock is prepared with a long sloping cut as flat as possible, i.e. with no twists. Ideally this cut is just the right depth into the wood so that when the scion is prepared with its whip cut, the two cambiums will be very close to each other – the stock and the scion and on both sides of the cuts. The whip cut aids the propagator who has to tie the cut in with polythene tape to exclude rain and pests, also to keep the union very tight and secure.

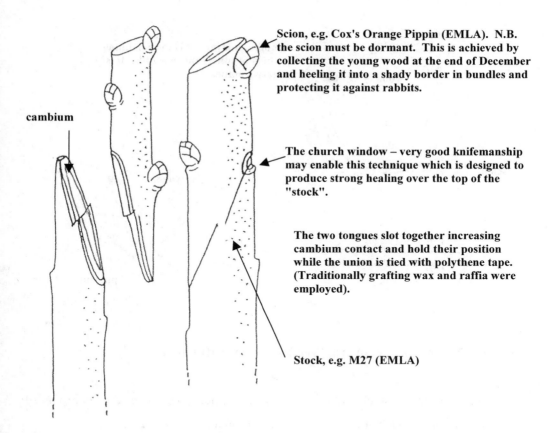

cambium

Scion, e.g. Cox's Orange Pippin (EMLA). N.B. the scion must be dormant. This is achieved by collecting the young wood at the end of December and heeling it into a shady border in bundles and protecting it against rabbits.

The church window – very good knifemanship may enable this technique which is designed to produce strong healing over the top of the "stock".

The two tongues slot together increasing cambium contact and hold their position while the union is tied with polythene tape. (Traditionally grafting wax and raffia were employed).

Stock, e.g. M27 (EMLA)

Figure 76: Whip and tongue grafting

Season – October to May, but usually c.February/March.

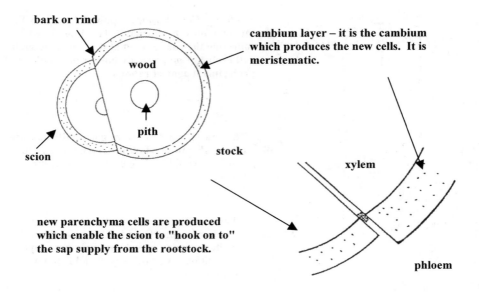

Figure 77: Young stem in cross-section at the graft union

The union of the rootstock and the scion comes about when the new cells produced by each cambium touch and work together to produce new tissues.

The production of new cells is associated with good growing conditions, i.e. ample oxygen, water and suitable temperature. These should all be close to optimum to ensure success.

Later, when the cambium has made a good bridge of callus tissue, new lignified xylem cells will be produced. These are the long wood fibres (vessels and tracheids) which will strengthen the graft union.

Wood is made up of these long cells. Examine a piece of wooden furniture – it may show the end grain – as in counting the annual rings, but it will probably also show where the wood was cut along the grain – along the length of the tree trunk or branch. Here the individual cells are long and overlap each other, providing both flexibility and strength.

(NB: The term 'grafting' is usually used where the scion has some woody length. There are many kinds of grafting, but most commonly practised is that known as 'whip and tongue' grafting. Other methods are saddle grafting, cleft grafting, crown grafting and budding – more correctly 'shield bud grafting' or chip budding.)

Shield Budding

There are various forms of budding, but that known as 'T' or shield budding and chip budding are the best known. Budding is usually carried out outdoors from the middle of July to the end of August. July and August are the best months for *Pyrus* and *Prunus* spp. Dull, showery weather is most suitable and apples and roses are common examples of plants that are budded.

i)   **Prepare rootstock (or stock)**

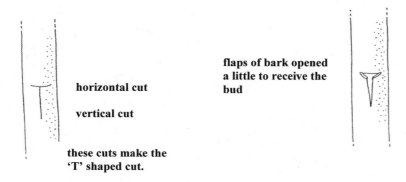

horizontal cut

vertical cut

flaps of bark opened a little to receive the bud

these cuts make the 'T' shaped cut.

Collect the bud wood as for chip budding.

ii) Preparing the bud

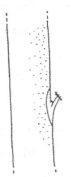

a short handle of the base of the leaf petiole

cut upwards to remove the (shield) bud

iii) The bud is inserted under the two flaps of bark and the top trimmed to the level of the horizontal cut.

bud inserted
and tied in

Figure 78: Budding (shield bud grafting or 'T' budding)

Bud stick preparation for rose:

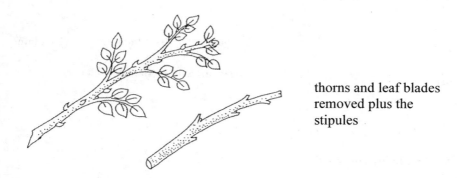

thorns and leaf blades
removed plus the
stipules

Use the long tail of rind to peel back and reveal the 'wood'. Peel out this sliver
carefully to leave the bud initials intact.

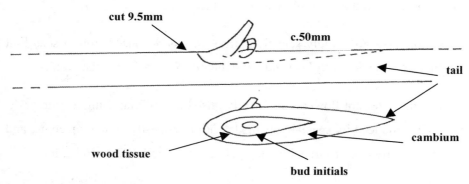

Figure 79: The 'shield' bud

Open the tips of the 'T' cut and insert the 'bud'. Push well down and trim off the
tail of the bud at the top of the 'T'. Tie in with a special tie bandage or raffia.

Seedling briars (root stocks), usually from stooled layers, are lined out in rows about
228mm x 762mm apart in the winter/spring prior to budding. They grow on in this
position during the summer. It would be usual to bud these stocks in July/August.

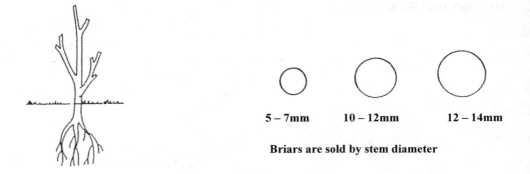

5 – 7mm   10 – 12mm   12 – 14mm

Briars are sold by stem diameter

Figure 80: The briar rootstock

The successfully budded briars are headed back carefully in late winter to remove all the briar top growth and to leave the implanted bud intact to grow out. This young shoot grows very rapidly and is best stopped at 150mm to encourage basal branching and reduce losses from the scion blowing out in the wind.

Rootstocks for roses are mainly selections from *R. canina* raised from a seed, but others such as *R. laxa, R. multiflora* and for standards *R. rugosa* are also used.

Roses under glass (for cut flowers) are mainly raised by grafting using a 'side graft' or a 'dovetail' produced by special cuts made with a modestly simple machine, and heated frames are used to ensure a high temperature for good callus production.

Side Veneer Grafting

'Green stick budding'

season July

Side graft, e.g. *Picea*

season February

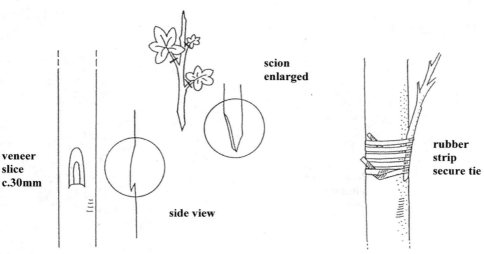

scion enlarged

veneer
slice
c.30mm

side view

rubber
strip
secure tie

Figure 81: Side veneer graft (e.g. *Acer palmatum***)**

Second year seedling of *Acer palmatum* about pencil thick - mid August. Care: 19°C for 7-10 days in very close, humid conditions. Thereafter more air and water pots sparingly. Release ties in about 2 weeks. Gradually begin to reduce the root stock head and when the growth begins to produce fresh leaves, the remainder of the head of the rootstock can be carefully 'headed back' to leave a minimal snag. Grow on under protection, e.g. polytunnel.

Figure 82: *Acer palmatum*
graft 'tied in'

Grafting onto Roots

This is a useful technique for some herbaceous plants and other species where the scion is fitted directly onto roots, e.g. herbaceous and tree paeony or wisteria.

Example: Clematis

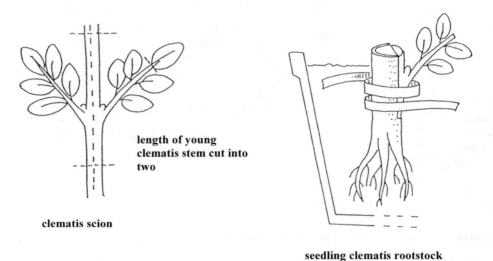

length of young clematis stem cut into two

clematis scion

seedling clematis rootstock

Figure 83: Two examples of root grafting

Example: Wisteria

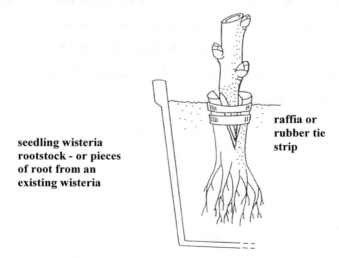

seedling wisteria rootstock - or pieces of root from an existing wisteria

raffia or rubber tie strip

(NB: This is rarely used now for clematis because with mist and fog plus very good growing conditions, specialist growers can raise excellent clematis from cuttings of short stem lengths with just one pair of buds, effectively a single node, wounded and hormone treated.)

BULBS AND CORMS

Scaling of Bulbs

In the case of narcissus and a number of other tunicate bulbs (where the leaf that makes up the bulb goes around the whole bulb like a tunic, e.g. an onion), there is a useful system of 'twin scaling' - though in practice there may be 3 or 4 such scale pieces.

The basis of the system is the basal stem of the bulb and the concept that in the axil of a leaf there is a bud. Well it seems that these bulbs have the capacity to generate a bud even where one is not actually obviously present.

Well-cleaned bulbs are divided into 8 to 10 vertical sections, each containing a part of the base plate (with its stem in effect). These sections are then sub-divided into segments with 3 or 4 scale pieces and not less than 2.

These sections are planted vertically into a prepared moist medium such as 50/50 peat and vermiculite, with their tips just showing. Alternatively, they may be kept jumbled up in a polybag of a similar mix of moist (but not wet) vermiculite and kept at 21°C for 3 to 8 weeks. In this period, bulblets are generated by the stem section at the base of the scale piece.

Cutting the *Narcissus* bulb into sections

(NB: Because this is actually big business - some purpose-built cutting machines have been manufactured.)

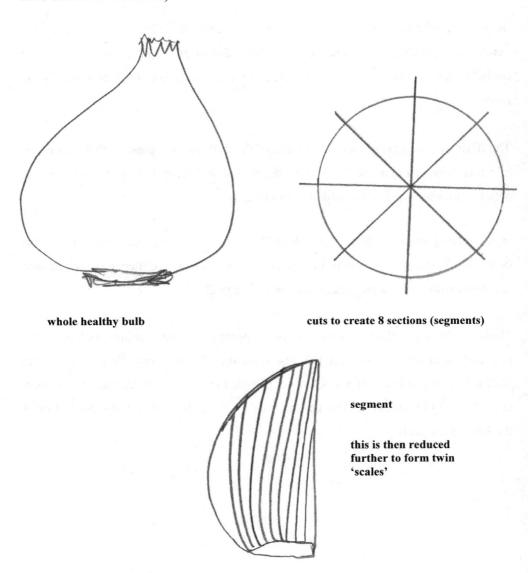

whole healthy bulb   cuts to create 8 sections (segments)

segment

this is then reduced
further to form twin
'scales'

Figure 84: Scaling of *Narcissus* bulb

A treatment with a fungicide may be helpful in preventing losses through rots caused by disease.

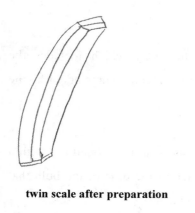

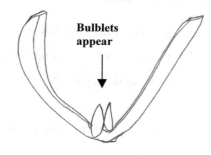

Bulblets
appear

twin scale after preparation

after the 3 to 8 week period in
moist vermiculite

These bulblets are then grown on in a nursery zone until they reach flowering size.

Many lilies, e.g. *Lilium longiflorum*, are scaly bulbs and may be broken up easily in November. These may be treated similarly to the narcissus twin scales. It is quite brilliant how the bulblets grow and after the spring/summer growing season in a nursery situation some bulbs will be large enough (15mm+) to flower the following year.

Leaf Scales

For example: *Lilium longiflorum, Lilium martagon, Lilium candidum* (the Madonna Lily)

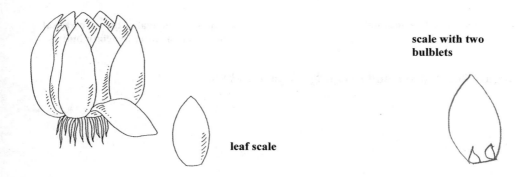

scale with two
bulblets

leaf scale

Figure 85 : Leaf scales – the modified leaves of an embrocate lily bulb

Scoring and Scooping

Hyacinths are the principal bulbs propagated in this way which includes the production of a large number of bulblets, vastly more than would come about by the natural sequence of division.

Large bulbs are selected in early summer and the basal plate is scooped out with a curved bladed knife. An alternative system scores across the base of the bulb that penetrate deeply into the bulb through the growing point.

The bulbs are dipped in fungicide and dusted with sulphur to combat decay. The bulbs are then allowed to callus in dry sand for a few days, cut side down.

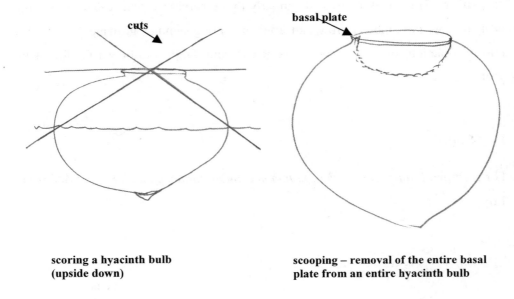

scoring a hyacinth bulb
(upside down)

scooping – removal of the entire basal
plate from an entire hyacinth bulb

Figure 86: Scoring and scooping a Hyacinth bulb

The Propagation of Corms

Important plants in this group are gladiolus and crocus. (It is harder to get cyclamen corms to multiply generously.)

A corm is a modified stem. Crocus and gladioli corms renew themselves annually. An external examination of a corm will show, starting at the bottom:

- the remains of last year's corm

- the external tunic, a covering protecting the corm from damage and water loss

- below the tunic may be seen a ring or several – which are the nodes

- an occasional lateral bud may be visible on the ring

- at the top of the corm may be a growth bud or several buds.

Gladioli and crocus will produce cormels (small corms) that may develop between the old and the new corms. Deep planting tends to increase the number of cormels produced. These cormels may be sifted out at lifting in the autumn and stored separately from the mother corms.

After lining out for a year, sown like seeds in drills, the size of the corm increases after the year's growth and some will be available to grade out for flower production and use. (Some of the cormels will flower in their first year but the stems are short and the season late.)

A warm bath treatment with a fungicide pre-planting is effective against fungal disorders.

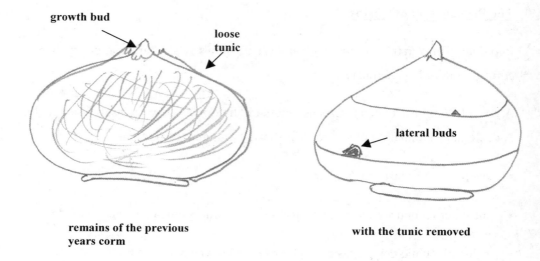

remains of the previous
years corm

with the tunic removed

The longitudinal section:

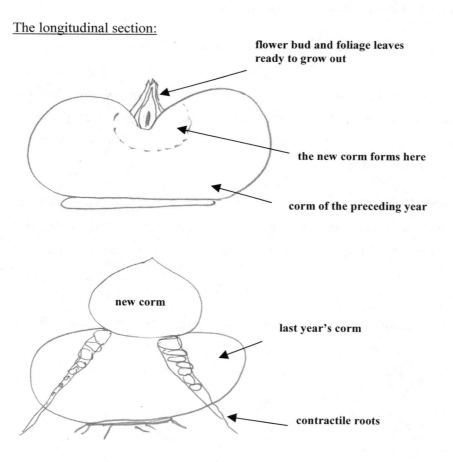

Figure 87: Crocus corm

PLANT NURSERY AND AFTERCARE

Following rooting, the young plants need nursery care so that they develop into strong plants.

With so many species, with their different needs, a simple care programme for all conditions is unlikely to say the least but there are areas which are common to all. These are the need for a suitable temperature, water, space (light), nutrients, oxygen and carbon dioxide and anchorage, plus freedom from competitors, poisons and excessive physical conditions (light, heat, cold, wind, relative humidity % and hail).

The text has largely endeavoured to be descriptive with details about the propagating phase and rather less on the protected cultivation – the period when the rooted material is pricked out, bedded out, potted up or lined out. To some extent these practical issues are included within the Practical Unit (Lesson 7) and later in the protected cropping text of Production Module D.

Maybe members might like to consider how to word a passage on the aftercare of plants for each of the following situations [and if I get too many saying "help please" I will write a supplementary passage of text as might seem appropriate - ONM]:

- a tender bedding plant seedling
- a tender species softwood cutting, or leaf cutting
- a hardy species softwood cutting, rooted and now in early June
- a hardy species semi-hardwood cutting, rooted and now in early September
- a direct stuck hardwood cutting, ex Garner bin and ready for its container and compost
- the treatment of layers of *Cotinus coggygria* cultivars on lifting in November of March
- splits of hardy herbaceous perennials like perennial asters in the winter and English bearded iris in July
- budded fruit stocks from 1st April
- conifers grafted under glass and polythene.

9. RISK ASSESSMENT

RELEVANT LEGISLATION

Section 2(3) of the Health and Safety at Work etc Act 1974 requires employers with five or more employees to prepare a written statement of their general policy on the health and safety at work of their employees. The Management of Health and Safety at Work (MHSW) Regulations 1992 require employers and the self-employed to identify significant hazards arising out of their work activities assess the risks and take steps to control those risks. If you employ five or more people you should record the significant findings of the assessment, i.e. those hazards which could result in serious injury or ill health, who is at risk from those hazards, what you are doing to control those hazards and what more (if anything) you need to do.

PREPARING A POLICY FOR HEALTH AND SAFETY

For further discussion of health and safety issues, see Section 9 "Risk Assessment, Safe Working Practices and Personal Protective Equipment (PPE)" in Module A, Lesson 3, Growing Media and Plant Nutrition of this course.

RISK ASSESSMENT

A Step-by-Step Approach to assessing risk:

1. Identify the hazards.

2. Identify those who might be harmed, and how.

3. Evaluate the risks arising from the hazards (is the risk high, medium or low?) and decide on measures and precautions to be taken.

4. Record assessment.

5. Periodically review and revise assessment.

ASPECTS OF HEALTH AND SAFETY IN PLANT PROPAGATION

Initially, it might appear that there are few operations that could cause any concern under the heading of Health and Safety in work concerned with propagation. However whether one is involved as an amateur gardener, employed as a professional gardener in a large garden, or in a management position there are a number of areas that must be addressed to endeavour to ensure that accidents do not occur. These include:

1. Poisonous seeds and plants - some, such as Lily-of-the-valley or *Ricinus* (Castor bean) are extremely poisonous, and plants such as *Dieffenbachia* (Dumb Cane) are so named for obvious reasons (do not chew it). Staff should wear gloves, or at least ensure that they wash their hands after handling such seeds / plant material.

2. Skin conditions and eczema - seeds of *Capsicum* (peppers) and leaves of some primulas can cause skin irritation, rashes and eczema in some workers. Rue can cause awful blisters and a speck of *Euphorbia* sap in the eye can cause hospitalisation.

3. The use of seed treatments and chemicals to treat seeds must be done with care (wearing masks, overalls and gloves according to the suppliers' instructions) and only at the recommended rates for use. Seed dressings and dusts can start an allergy or attacks of asthma. Also mites may be present on seeds, bulbs, corms and dry roots.

4. The rooting powders used are hormone based in talc or dissolved in alcohol, so avoid breathing them in unnecessarily. Some may have fungicidal pesticides included as a part of their formulation.

5. Electrical equipment used in propagation frames as warming cables, as mist propagation or any heating, lighting or irrigation controls should be installed and serviced by a qualified electrician.

The risks to safety are high with the power used in association with so many moist surfaces and running water, if insulation is less than in good repair.

6. Handling heavy loads must now be considered. Training for staff is usual in many organisations. Use lifting gear and mechanisation for large deliveries of such items as bags of compost.

7. Sharp knives, secateurs, loppers and saws all have potential to cause injury. Adequate, careful training and good operational procedures can help hugely in avoiding accidents.

8. Keep a fully stocked First Aid kit available, and make sure everyone knows its location. Keep an accident book and have an agreed procedure in case of accidents. Arrange First Aid training. Wear the correct protective clothing for the job!

Overall in propagation work try and be aware of the possible dangers and think about what you are doing. Proper use of all equipment and machinery, together with a little thought about others around you (including children and visitors generally, all of whom may choose to poke about, smell bottles, open this and that and check the sharpness of your saws, etc.) will all help to avoid anyone getting hurt.

DISCLAIMER

Whilst every effort has been taken by the Horticultural Correspondence College (HCC) to ensure the accuracy of the information in the lesson pages, the HCC wishes to emphasise that the contents in the lessons are regularly reviewed and are naturally subject to change from time to time. The HCC also give notice that it will not accept liability for any inaccuracies within this book. As the text information is regularly reviewed, the HCC would welcome any comments.

Our authors acknowledge the value of reference material now in the public domain and available off the internet.

The aim of this book is to provide an overall guide to the content of the RHS Advanced (Module A) syllabus by giving notes and diagrams on the basic underlying principles and how these can be adopted and used in actual propagation of plants. There are further details on the propagation of named subject and also a list of sources from which the student may obtain more information and extend his or her range of background knowledge.

Hopefully this will enable the studious reader to complete the text programme satisfactorily to pass the Module A written paper of The Royal Horticultural Society Advanced General Certificate in Horticulture.

FOUR SET QUESTIONS

These questions and specimen answers are intended to be helpful parts of this book and typical of the material in the course from which this text has been derived.

N.B. – Please do not send in written work.

[Note : Where appropriate include **one** diagram only]

QUESTION ONE

Compare the methods of using mist propagation with warm bench and plastic floating film or tenting. Briefly, what are the advantages and the disadvantages, if any? Illustrate one system.

QUESTION TWO

Describe two different grafting methods used in the propagation of named plants of hardy nursery stock.

QUESTION THREE

Describe and discuss five ideal characteristics and factors which you would take into account when selecting material for cuttings.

QUESTION FOUR

Plant propagation is not just about rooting material, it is also a question of achieving a quality, independent plant – hence this Question 4 :

The propagation unit, consisting of a mist unit, a "wet" fog unit, a heated bench, together with some nursery land, has a nominal production per crop:

- 5,000 rooted softwood stem cuttings (of hardy woody ornamentals)
- 500 rooted leaf cuttings of *Begoniaceae* and *Gesneriaceae*
- 5,000 lily scales
- 10 trays of bedding geranium F_1 hybrid seeds at c.120 seedlings per tray.

a) Discuss the area of bench space required for:

  (i) the rooting phase for each crop

  (ii) the space needed after the first move (e.g. into 100mm pots) and state what containers would be required.

b) (i) What potting media would you choose for each crop?

  (iii) What environmental provisions would be necessary for each (assume the date is mid-April)?

c) State what would happen next for each crop and approximately when this would be.

d) What percentage of genuine useful propagating space would you expect to be available in a mist house 10m x 15m?

[NB : The specimen answer includes a discussion which is wider than the question's actual remit]

TEN SHORT ANSWER QUESTIONS

[Note: DO NOT SEND in your answers to these 10 questions – the specimen answers are supplied]

1.   What do you understand by dormancy as it relates to seed?

2.   Give 2 examples of seeds with natural dormancy characteristics.

3.   Describe 2 methods of breaking seed dormancy for difficult seeds.

4.   What is the tissue that produces the callus at the base of a cutting?

5.   For a named plant which of the following 5 methods of plant propagation could be used:

   (i)   seed

   (ii)   cuttings

   (iii)   layering

   (iv)   division

   (v)   grafting

6.   Name a disease that could reduce the germination success of bedding plants.

7.   Name a disease affecting the successful taking of cuttings.

8.   Name of mollusc pest.

9.   Name an insect pest.

10.   Name a seed subject to the risk of virus infection.

REFERENCE SOURCES AND SUGGESTED READING

The Landsman's Bookshop at Buckenhill, Bromyard, Herefordshire, issues an excellent catalogue of books and pamphlets on all aspects of horticulture and propagation. If you can have access to the internet, their website is www.landsmans.co.uk. Also, Amazon Books supplier website, www.amazon.co.uk or Books Online website, www.uk.bol.com, which helps you to trace a book, or one on a particular topic, often at below the normal high street prices.

The following books were available in print at August 2000:

Applied Principles of Horticultural Science. L. Brown
Publisher: Butterworth-Heinmann, August 1996. ISBN Number 0750629541

Grafter's Handbook.
Ward Lock paperback, Jan 1993. ISBN Number 0304342742

Hillier's Manual of Trees and Shrubs.
Publisher: David and Charles hardback, 1991.

Modern Plant Propagation. Allan Gardine
Publisher: Lothian Books, Aug. 1989. ISBN Number 0850912830

Nursery Stock Manual. (Grower Manual 1) K. Lamb, J. Kelly & P. Bowbrick
Publisher: Grower Books. Revised May 1998. ISBN Number 1899372040

Plant Propagation. K. Hartmann
Publisher: Prentice Hall hardcover Dec.1996. ISBN Number 0132061031

Plant Propagation. Philip Macmillan Browse
Publisher: Royal Horticultural Society
Michael Beazley paperback, 1999. ISBN Number 1840001569

Plant Propagation made easy: The Complete Guide to Raising Hardy, Tender and Indoor Plants. Alan Toogood
Publisher: Timber Press, 1989. ISBN Number 088192279X

Plant Propagation by Tissue Culture in Practice. E.F. George
1996 ISBN Number 0950932558

Practical Woody Plant Propagation for Nursery Growers. Bruce Macdonald
Publisher: Timber Press, 1989. ISBN Number 0881920622

Principles of Horticulture. C.R. Adams, K. M. Bamford and M. P. Early
Publisher: Butterworth – Heinmann, 1998. ISBN Number 075064043X

The Complete Book of Plant Propagation. J. Arbury, R. Bird and C. Innes
Publisher: Mitchell Beazley hardback, 1997. ISBN Number 1857327535

The Guide to Successful Propagation. Alistair Ayers (Editor)
Publisher: Which Books hardback, 1995.

[P.S. Many of the references and diagrams for this text came from Oliver Menhinick's own modest book, Plant Propagation Insight Fundamentals and Techniques, published in 1994, but now out of print.]

STUDIES TOWARDS THE
RHS ADVANCED GENERAL CERTIFICATE IN HORTICULTURE

MODULE A - LESSON 1

PLANT PROPAGATION

SPECIMEN ANSWERS

- **QUESTION ONE**

Compare the methods of using (a) mist propagation with (b) warm bench and plastic (floating film and/or tenting) propagation. Briefly, what are the advantages and the disadvantages, if any? Illustrate one system.

Answer:

(a)   Mist Propagation

Generally this involves an area of protected space devoted to the purpose because of pipework, control systems and heating requirements. The cost per m^2 for mist is very considerable - £100 m^2 plus for a fairly small unit.

Mist is brilliant for rooting leafy softwood cuttings in the spring and summer months when it prevents desiccation of the cuttings, has a cooling effect on leaves, reduces air temperatures in the hottest months and cuts down the respiration rate so that the cuttings use up less of their carbohydrate reserves. Rooting may be very speedy and the rooted cutting is very soon seeking supplementary nutrition.

Mist propagation can often cause the failure of cuttings during the winter months due to becoming excessively wet, making the control of fungal diseases a problem. Some use of intermittent mist can overcome this difficulty. Subjects with hairy leaves will often rot under mist but, with polythene only, success is more assured.

(b)   Warm Bench and Plastic

This is essentially a much cheaper system because it does not require as much equipment – no water pump, filtration (maybe with nitric acid treatment for the water's pH adjustment) and electrical sensing/timing devices.

In essence the bench is likely to be arranged over existing heated pipework. It is important to get the heating right and careful temperature measurement to ensure that an even temperature within the optimum rooting temperature range is achieved.

Hygiene is very important and the use of fungicides may be an essential tool to assure production and good crop quality.

During winter months cuttings under polythene without mist appear to be more successful. The system is less expensive to operate and there is less leaching of hormones and nutrients from the cuttings.

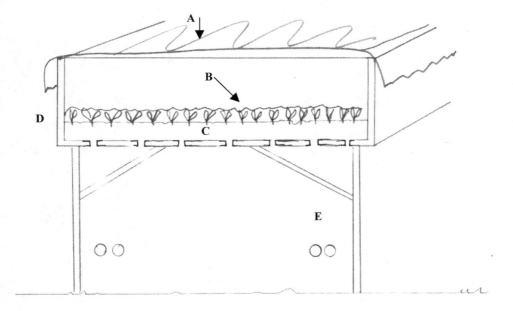

Illustration of Warm bench and plastic

Key:

A =   roll of heavy duty, milky film polythene with additional shade roll material available to supplement shade

B =   floating film of lightweight clear polythene sitting on the wet foliage of the leafy cuttings

C =   the rooting medium, e.g. 50/50 peat and grit

D =   the Warm Bench itself – maybe 2m wide, 300mm deep and 1m to the top in height

E =   High speed hot water pipes – or other heating system – a soil warming system is desirable.

- **QUESTION TWO**

Describe two different grafting methods used in the propagation of named plants of hardy nursery stock.

Answer:

Side Veneer Grafting

A range of plants are propagated by veneer grafts, including:

- *Fagus sylvatica* cultivars onto *F.sylvatica* seedlings

- *Picea pungens* cultivars onto *P. pungens* seedlings

- *Picea abies* cultivars onto *P. abies* seedlings

- *Cedrus atlantica* cultivars onto *C. atlantica* seedlings

- *Acer platanoides* 'Crimson King' onto *A. platanoides* seedlings

These are bench grafted – i.e. the grafting of the rootstocks is carried out onto potted (or, in some cases, bare root) rootstocks. These grafts can be carried out between December and February, also in July/August. The rootstocks are housed (in a glasshouse or similar) and encouraged to make some new root – 2-3 weeks at 10-15°C.

They should be dry at the roots, i.e. not wet. There is a real risk that excessive sap will be produced at the cuts made in grafting and this reduces the success. Make the grafts, tie in and wax (grafting wax provides a waterproof and supportive protective coating). Alternatively, and very commonly used, a range of tie materials are available including short length of rubber elastic, which work extremely well, also polythene ties. Ties should be removed at an early date after it is quite clear that the graft has taken and is secure.

Plunge the grafted stocks in a moist peat bed at 20°C with an air temperature of c.15-18°C in a very high humidity. Spray overhead. Cover the stocks with a poly tent or drape. Shade is required. Restrict watering until the buds swell. After 6-8 weeks head back the stock to half its length and again to 25mm above the union in late summer when the union is completely secure.

Side veneer graft

(e.g. of *Betula pendula* 'Dalecarlica' onto 3 year old seedlings of *B.pendula*)

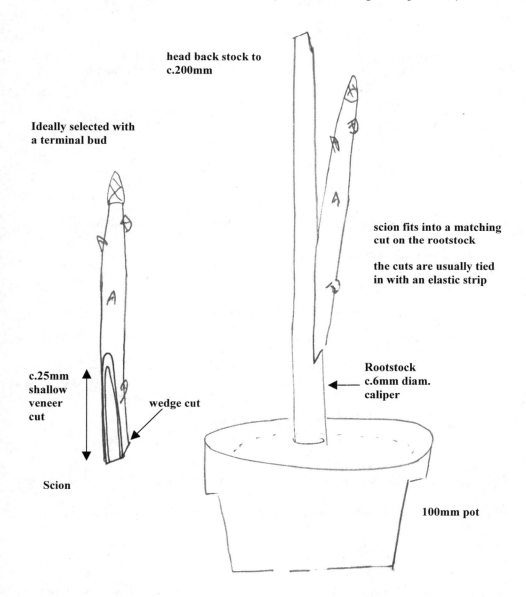

head back stock to c.200mm

Ideally selected with a terminal bud

scion fits into a matching cut on the rootstock

the cuts are usually tied in with an elastic strip

c.25mm shallow veneer cut

wedge cut

Rootstock c.6mm diam. caliper

Scion

100mm pot

Budding Bush Roses

Bud stick preparation for rose:

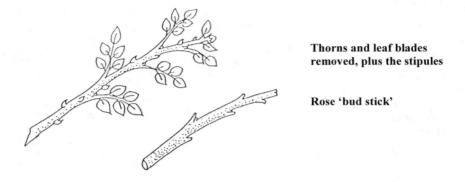

Thorns and leaf blades removed, plus the stipules

Rose 'bud stick'

Use the long tail of rind to peel back and reveal the 'wood'. Peel out this sliver carefully to leave the bud initials intact.

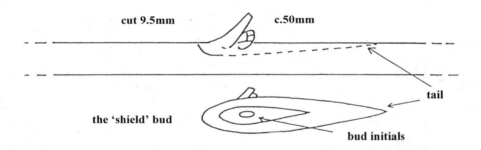

Open the lips of the 'rind' at the 'T' cut and insert the 'bud'. Push well down and trim off the tail of the bud at the top of the 'T'. Tie in with a special tie bandage or raffia.

Seedling briars (rootstocks) – usually imported as seedlings c.8-10mm in circumference - are lined out in rows about 228mm x 762mm (9" x 30") apart in the winter/spring prior to budding.

They grow on in this position during the summer. It would be usual to bud these stocks in July/August.

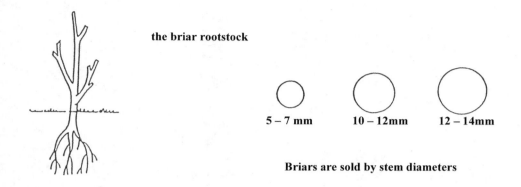

the briar rootstock

5 – 7 mm   **10 – 12mm**   **12 – 14mm**

Briars are sold by stem diameters

The successfully budded briars are headed back carefully in late winter to remove all the briar top growth.

The buds grow out rapidly in April and this young shoot should be stopped at c.200-250mm in length – they are very apt to 'blow out' otherwise in windy times. The stopping also assists the development of several strong basal stems, which become the initial framework of the bush rose at the end of the growing season. When the bushes are lifted, cut back to c.150mm and plant in their final growing position.

Budding Standard Roses

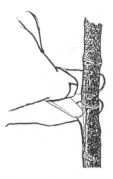

'T' shaped cut

removing the bud from the bud stick

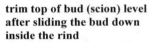

cut level with the 'T' cut

trim top of bud (scion) level
after sliding the bud down
inside the rind

Wrapping the bud to secure.
Leave the bud itself visible
With this sort of tape tie.

place 3 buds
equidistant at
the chosen
height, e.g.
c.1m from
ground level

Standard briar

- **QUESTION THREE**

Describe and discuss 5 ideal characteristics and factors which you would take into account when selecting material for cuttings.

Answer:

Growers should always aim to produce high quality stock. This starts by sourcing material which is true to type, free from pests and diseases, in vigorous growth, and is correctly labelled.

1. Trueness to type means that it is the correct genus, species or cultivar and that flower colour, growth, habit and all such other characteristics match the description of the particular plant you are growing.

2. One of the most important aspects to consider is that all newly introduced stock is free from viruses – which can cause depressed growth, little or no flowering, few fruit, and malformed leaves. Freedom from fungal and bacterial infections also matters, as well as freedom from pests present on or within the material (e.g. chrysanthemum eelworm).

3. Plant vigour is essential and this is maintained by having a stock of young plants linked to a regular programme of fertilisation, pruning to encourage healthy, new vegetation and regular control of any pests. This juvenile wood is much easier to propagate than that collected from old branches – as may be necessary when plant hunting in the wild. It is often advisable to keep stock plants separate from the rest of the nursery production to ensure that their labelling is not muddled and to maintain freedom from infection.

4. The size and shape of the material is significant. While the most vigorous shoots may root well they may also be more subject to losses from disease and the thinnest shoots may produce plants of less vigour. In practice, a hedge row approach may be the most attractive to choose because of the strong laterals with uniform qualities. It is good practice to avoid collecting cutting material from ground level (in the rain-splashed mud zone) to reduce the chance of infection from soil-borne pathogens. It can matter enormously whether the cutting has a terminal bud as its absence may deprive plants (of some species) forever of having a central stem with balanced growth around it.

5. Within the question there is the word "when" and this is part of the important factors in that early cuttings of deciduous softwood stem cuttings may be much more successful as plants and in overwintering because they will have had a longer growing season – rooted early they will have had more growing days.

    For deciduous hardwood cuttings there is a curious cycle of rooting potential. This starts higher – at its best for many species - at the close of the growing season and tends to drop badly in December and January with a very short period of excellent rooting potential in the period immediately prior to the rise of sap in the spring. In effect this means that a routine of taking cuttings in October and November is very sensible, but that some cuttings taken late can be also be a great success – especially if there is rooting hormone and a 'Garner' bin'available. Once the buds have begun to swell or burst the chance of rooting is almost completely gone.

•   **QUESTION FOUR**

Plant propagation is not just about rooting material, it is also a question of achieving a quality, independent plant – hence this Question 4:

The propagation unit, consisting of a mist unit, a "wet" fog unit, a heated bench together with some nursery land, has a nominal production per crop:

- 5,000 rooted softwood stem cuttings (of hardy woody ornamentals)
- 500 rooted leaf cuttings of *Begoniaceae* and *Gesneriaceae*
- 5,000 lily scales
- 10 trays of bedding geranium F_1 hybrid seeds at c.120 seedlings per tray.

a)   Discuss the area of bench space required for:
      (i)   the rooting phase for each crop
      (ii)   the space needed after the first move (e.g. into 100mm pots) and state what containers would be required.
b)   (i)   What potting media would you chose for each crop?
      (ii)   What environmental provisions would be necessary for each (assume the date is mid-April)?
c)   State what would happen next for each crop and approximately when this would be.
d)   What percentage of genuine useful propagating space would you expect to be available in a mist house 10m x 15m ?

[NB: The specimen answer includes a discussion, which is wider than the question's actual remit.]

Answer: [Please see notes on Question 4 on page 214.]

a) (i) The space required for the rooting phase of:

- 5,000 softwood stem cuttings. If each cutting is placed at 50mm square, the area required is $12.5m^2$ of mist bench.

- 500 leaf cuttings spaced as above = $1.25m^2$.

- 5,000 lily leaf scales. These need only be in a polybag mixed in with vermiculite. Say at 200 scales per bag of c.2 litres volume, there would need to be space for 25 bags of 2 litres – which could be accommodated easily in $1m^2$.

- (germination of)10 trays of geranium seeds = c.1m^2. (Or, to be more precise, 0.8m^2).

a) (ii) The space, and containers, required after the first move:

- 5,000 rooted 'liners' in 100mm pots would require 50m^2 of heated bench space.

- 500 leaf cuttings in 100mm pots would require 5m^2 of heated benching.

- 5,000 lily leaf scales, now containerised into deep growing boxes (flats) and placed at c.50 x 50mm = 12.5m^2.

- 10 trays of bedding plants – say 1,000 good seedlings in 20 cell plastic trays = 50 seed trays needed = c.4 m^2 of bench space.

b) (i) The potting media for:

- Rooting the softwoods – 50/50 peat/grit.

- Leaf cuttings – a JIP1 type mix or a loamless mix to include nutrients.

- Lily leaf scales – a loamless mix.

- 10 trays of bedding geraniums – JIP1 or a loamless mix.

b) (ii) Environmental conditions in mid-April:

Plant Material	Temperature °C	Relative Humidity %	Light/Dark
Rooted softwood stem cuttings	c.15 - 18	c.80	Full light
Rooted leaf cuttings	22 - 25	c.90	Good light but sunless
Lily leaf scales (in flats)	15 – 18	50 – 60	Full light
Seedling germination	18 – 20	60 – 70	Full light

c) What happens next and when:

- The softwood stem cuttings could be containerised into a loamless GCRI type of proprietary potting mix. The date for this could be 8-10 weeks after 'making the cuttings'.

- The new begonia and gesneria plants are now potted. They will be able to grow on to form luxuriant plants needing ample liquid feed and ample space.

- The lily leaf scales may be planted outside in nursery rows in the following April.

- The geranium seedlings will have developed to a fair size and produced a flower. It would have been possible to treat them with a growth retardant so that they developed a more bushy habit. This does delay the crop but the plant becomes much more effective as a bedding plant early on in the summer bedding scheme with its extra 'breaks' – the flowering stems. With a late crop of seedlings they would be useful in 'pot bedding' to replace a late season of Sweet Williams or to replace a crop of, say, 10 week stocks which had finished flowering.

d) It can be remarkable just how much space is lost to paths and access. The advantage of mobile benching may be to economise in the use of available space.

- For the 10m x 5m mist house with fixed benches:

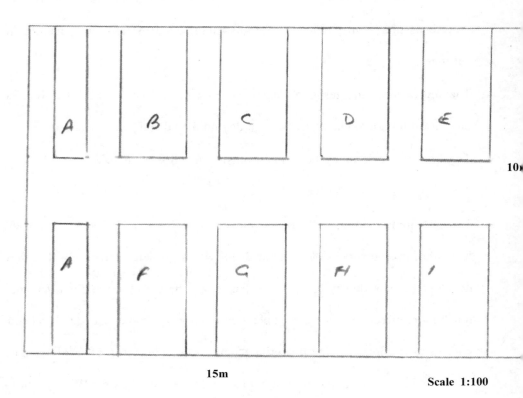

15m

Scale 1:100

2No. beds **A** @ 4 x 1m = 8m² ⎫
                                       ⎬ Total bench space
8No. beds **B** to **I** @ 4 x 2m = 64m² ⎭ = 72 m²

Area of house = 150m²

Percentage area of productive space: 72 / 150 x 100 = 48 %

- For the 10m x 5m mist house with mobile benches:

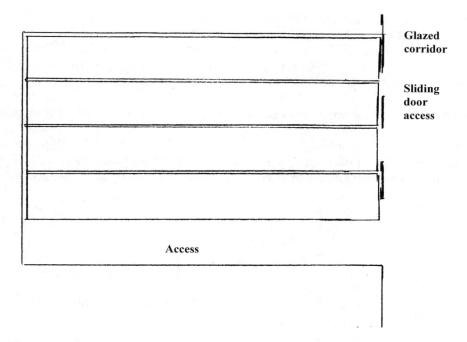

With mobile benching each bench is able to roll sideways by about one-third of its width. This enables the path space to move.

In the above illustration, which is possible if the end of the propagating house is accessed from a glazed corridor or covered working area, the useful space is:

4No. beds @ 15 x 2m wide = 120m^2 total bench space.

120 / 150 x 100 = 80%

If the most important path can be relieved from its role in transportation of the crop, by using an overhead gantry system, the percentage of useful space could go up to 90% - almost double the area of the fixed bench system.

Notes on Question 4 (a)

This is a straight calculation question. If possible, measure a professional seed tray and calculate how much space 10 seed trays will require.

"Our" seed tray measured 228 x 348mm. Therefore 22.8cm x 34.8cm = 793.44cm^2 x 10 trays = 7,934.4cm^2 x 5 (for 50 trays) = 39,672cm^2. Divide by 1m^2 to give area of bench space required, i.e. 39,672 / 10,000 = 3.96m^2 (c.4m^2).

As a basis for calculation, it might be useful to put the 5000 liners into 100mm pots.

It is quite straightforward to measure the length by the breadth and multiply up the space required by so many pots or seed trays. Round pots placed pot thick can be set square to one another, which is more usual than the tighter squeezed offset pattern.

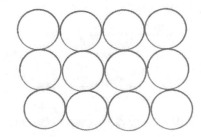

Pot thick – on the square

(The more usual choice)

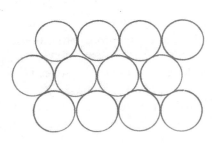

While, on the face of it, this question is difficult, it is not intended to be and anyone with green fingers and a small greenhouse will know that the surface area is finite to the extent that there is no space left.

In question 4 (d) the mist house will have to have paths and access space. In effect this is not useful space for actual propagation. So, if half of the mist propagating house is paths there is only 50% left of genuine useful propagating space and the calculation becomes clear.

Mobile benches are a method of reducing the area occupied by fixed paths, but there is no need to go to these lengths to answer this question.

A calculation question is quite a probability in our view. The Specimen Answer does provide a wider discussion than is strictly required.

TEN SHORT ANSWER QUESTIONS

Q1 What do you understand by dormancy as it relates to seed?
A Viable seed may not germinate if it has a mechanism which has evolved over time and which prevents germination unless some specific conditions are met to break the dormancy.

Q2 Give 2 examples of seeds with natural dormancy characteristics.
A (i) Oily seed coats as in magnolia
(ii) Lettuce seed which will not germinate if the temperature is too high, e.g. 20°C.

Q3 Describe 2 methods of breaking seed dormancy for difficult seeds.
A (i) Stratification by winter chilling for woody species, e.g. *Malus, Ilex, Rosa*.
(ii) Scarification to puncture, crack or reduce the thickness of the seed Coat, e.g. *Prunus*.

Q4 What is the tissue that produces the callus at the base of a cutting?
A Cambium.

Q5 For a named plant which of the following 5 methods of plant propagation could be used?
(i) seed
(ii) cuttings
(iii) layering
(iv) division
(v) grafting
A For example – *Malus floribunda*:
(i) OK for the species
(ii) OK for hardwood cuttings in Garner Bins
(iii) From stooled layers
(iv) From stooled layers in extreme circumstances
(v) OK for 'T' budding, chip budding and whip and tongue.

Q6 Name a disease which could reduce the germination success of bedding plants.
A *Pythium* – a damping off disease.

Q7   Name a disease affecting the successful taking of cuttings.

A   There are important members in the group of diseases affecting cuttings, including:

Rhizoctonia, Phytophthora, Ascochyta, Glomerella, Cylindrocladium, Botrytis, Fusarium, Verticillium.

Q8   Name a mollusc pest.

A   A slug, e.g. the Grey field slug.

Q9   Name an insect pest.

A   An aphid, e.g. the Peach potato aphid.

Q10   Name a seed subject to the risk of virus infection.

A   Tomato
Lettuce
Cucumber.